MAKING THE INTERNET WORK FOR YOUR BUSINESS

Angela Booth

ALLEN & UNWIN

First published in 1999 by
Allen & Unwin
9 Atchison Street, St Leonards NSW 1590, Australia
Phone: (61 2) 8425 0100
Fax: (61 2) 9906 2218
E-mail: frontdesk@allen-unwin.com.au
Web: http://www.allen-unwin.com.au

National Library of Australia
Cataloguing-in-Publication entry:

Booth, Angela, 1949– .
  Making the internet work for your business.

  Includes index.
  ISBN 1 86448 738 0.

  1. Small business—Computer networks. 2. Internet
  (Computer network). 3. World Wide Web (Information
  retrieval system). 4. Internet marketing. I. Title.

658.0546

Set in 11/13.5 pt Bembo by DOCUPRO, Sydney
Printed by Australian Print Group, Maryborough, Victoria

10 9 8 7 6 5 4 3 2 1

Contents

What can the Internet do for your business?

The Internet is a giant computer network, connecting millions of computers and their users right around the world, and it can revolutionise your business. The global computer network means that you can get more done in less time, at a lower cost. For most small businesses, the biggest benefit is that your customers can learn about your products and services simply and quickly, at any hour of the day or night, no matter where they are in the world. When you make information accessible in this way, it can turn a customer into a friend—a friend who wants to do business with you. It can even change a customer's perception of your business.

For example, last week I spent twenty minutes on the phone, on hold, to a courier company. As the minutes ticked by, I got angrier and angrier. This company was now on my list of 'Companies I Will Never Do Business With Again'. The parcel I was waiting for was three days overdue, and the item it contained was expensive. The company I'd purchased the item from (via the Internet) swore that the courier company had picked up the parcel for overnight delivery three days ago. Then crackling over the phone line I heard: '*If you have an Internet connection, we provide a parcel tracking service. Just go to our Internet address at—*'

I put the phone down and clicked on my Internet connection. I typed the courier company's Internet address into my browser, and the company's home page loaded quickly. I typed in the parcel's docket number, and within 30 seconds was rewarded with a screenful of information. The last line gave the date, told me my parcel had been loaded at 6.50am, and was on board Van UA2345 for delivery that afternoon. The parcel duly arrived that afternoon. By making information I needed easily available, my perception of the courier company changed.

Whatever your business, an Internet connection will help you to do more business, no matter how you choose to use your online connection—whether you build a full-blown interactive Web site, which allows you to take orders online, or whether you put up a simple page with your business's name and a map of your location. One of the best definitions of selling I've ever heard is: *selling is relating*. The Internet helps you to relate to people.

FOUR BENEFITS OF THE INTERNET FOR YOUR BUSINESS

1 The Internet saves you precious time. A Web site can act as a 24-hour salesperson.
2 The Internet provides cheap and easy communications. You don't need to print out letters or faxes. You save a lot of money on local mail, and even more on international mail. You also extend the reach of your business. Your potential marketplace becomes global, rather than local. You'll find that because online communications are so easy, you'll communicate more. Customers you previously contacted with a mailing once every six to twelve months, you'll contact by e-mail with a notice of your current specials once a month. More frequent contact leads to more business.
3 The Internet saves you the costs of premises and staff. You can maintain an electronic shop (a Web site) located completely in cyberspace. Your 'virtual' store is open 24 hours, it needs no staff, and anyone in the world with access to a computer can visit it.
4 You'll save on many other costs. Advertising costs are a good example. If an ad in your local paper is costing you $100 a week, that's $100 saved. At the same time, you are dramatically extending your business's reach way beyond your local area. You'll also save on costs like providing after-sales service, and buying mailing lists

—the Internet means that you can create your own targeted lists online.

Let's look more closely at these benefits.

The Internet saves you precious time

One of the benefits of the Internet is that it works, even when you're not at work. It allows you to provide a service that operates seven days a week, 24 hours a day. When you provide enough information about your products, you can let your clients do most of the work for you.

Lin Andrews, of the South Australian real estate company Lin Andrews Real Estate, tells of the client who accessed his company Web site late on a Saturday night. Lin says: 'The people who find us

The Lin Andrews Real Estate—the site sells every day of the year.

on the Internet tend to be independent types. He searched our online database, and found a property he was interested in. We provide photos on the site, so he saved those to his computer, along with the floorplan of the house.' Lin laughs and shakes his head as he goes on to say: 'He walked around the property on Sunday morning, then called me at home on Sunday night, and signed the contract at our office on the Monday morning.'

If you're thinking that this situation was a one-off occurrence, Lin assures you that it's not unusual:

> Last month I sold two beachfront properties within a day of each other to people who found them on our Web site. We'd listed both properties for a year offline without finding buyers for them, but they sold within weeks of being listed on the Web. The properties sold with minimal client interaction and contact.

Kevin Clay is another person who believes that the Internet is great for real estate agents. Kevin is the chair of the board of REALNET, an online service of the Real Estate Agents Cooperative, with member agents in New South Wales, Queensland, Western Australia and New Zealand. According to Kevin, the Internet extends Australian real estate agents' market globally:

> We have frequent sales to overseas clients. They find the property they're interested in online. Many never come to Australia; they buy the property on the basis of online information. As early as 1996 we received a letter from a gentleman in Thailand. He was interested in a house in Rydalmere (NSW), however it had been sold by the time we heard from him. He went on to buy another property that we listed online, for around $200 000.

By eliminating the need for lengthy communications with clients, the Internet saves time for real estate agents—it can save time for you in your business as well.

The Internet provides cheap, easy communications

Any SOHO (Small Office Home Office) business operator is always looking for new ways to trim margins. An Internet connection will save you big money in communications costs: you can cut down on postage charges, and you'll have fewer phone charges. You'll also save on paper and printing costs. And because you can provide as much information as they need *cheaply* to your prospective clients, you're likely to make more sales, particularly of large-ticket items.

Used efficiently, the Internet is a communications medium which can turbo-charge a sluggish business. When you use the Internet for your business, there are no slow times. You don't need to wait for your customers to come to you. We'll discuss how you can find business online, via online discussion lists and online advertising, later in the book. These tools will cost you nothing except your time.

Your Internet shopfront is open around the clock, communicating with your customers (potential and current) and your suppliers. You can communicate with them in real time. That is, when your customers access your Web site, they can get information about your goods and services, and prices, and they can place orders. If they have questions, they can send you a message, and you'll be able to respond to their questions promptly—usually within a few hours. You can even set up a complete e-commerce system on your site. E-commerce basically means using your Web site as a merchant commerce system. This means handling orders, payment, and fulfilment via the site. As you might imagine, this can be complex, and it's best to get professional advice from a Web site development company. For useful information on e-commerce, check out the Sell It On the Web site, at URL: http://sellitontheweb.com.

One of the most exciting features of the World Wide Web is that it's a multimedia experience; not only can your customers see your product and read about it, they can also hear about the product, and watch the product in action via video.

Mark Woschnak of RealWeb, another online service for real estate agents, believes the RealWeb's Web site makes it possible to provide information for consumers which it would be impractical to provide in any other way. Agents who are members of RealWeb can present large amounts of information on each property:

> There are four pages of information for each property. The first page offers a photo and description, as well as the agent's contact details. The next page offers the interior and exterior features of the property: number of bathrooms, pool, etc. The third page features the financial details: the price, the lease if there is one, the rates and other outgoings. The last page can contain up to six more photos, and up to eight more documents relating to the property, such as the contract, a floorplan—whatever the agent wishes to include.

Traditional communication involves paper—letters, faxes, flyers, brochures, price lists, and so on. One of the biggest money-saving features of a Web site is that it helps you to climb out from underneath a mass of paper—product specifications, catalogues, brochures and leaflets, and the associated printing and mailing costs of all of these. Harold Malewski, of the mail-order firm Trend Sportswear, now sells women's clothing from a virtual shopfront on the World Wide Web. He has no printed catalogue, and he estimates that this saves him around $40 000 a year. He did experience an initial resistance—his customers wanted a printed catalogue! However, he had no plans to print one. So he placed a notice on his Web site stating that 'no trees were harmed in the creation of this site. Please print out product images, descriptions and your order form'. He says that the low overheads of his online site have helped him to keep his business afloat in tough times.

Harold believes that e-mail is another money-saver for his business, although he hasn't tried to estimate how much he saves with it. He says:

> E-mail is painless communication. There's no envelope or stamp to find, there's no trip to the post office. I use e-mail for market research. I send out e-mail questionnaires as soon as a new catalogue goes up on my Web site. The customers hit the Reply button, fill in the questionnaire, and then hit the Send button. We know what will sell because we ask. We know why women buy our clothes and when they wear them. At the end of a season we don't end up with a warehouse full of clothes which didn't sell.

As Harold does, you can use cheap online communications as a market-research tool. Market research in the physical world is expensive. In the online world, however, your customers can get information to you as easily as you can provide information to them. In the physical world, you need to create, print and mail out questionnaires. You need to give your customers an incentive to fill out the questionnaires and return them to you. Market research online is as simple as adding a questionnaire to your Web site. It's inexpensive, and the results are almost instantaneous. For example, you can create an e-mail questionnaire of five or ten questions, and most respondents will get them back to you the same day. This allows you to finetune your business—you can see instantly what's working and what's not. And if something is not working, you can find out why.

Another benefit is that you'll be able to locate the people who are interested in your product or service, and who want to do business with you *now*. You can forget direct postal mail campaigns which cost you a small fortune, and which don't give you a good return on your investment. On the Internet, you can classify your prospects narrowly—in fact, your prospects will classify themselves.

As well as postal and printing charges, and phone and fax bills, the Internet can also save you travel time. For example, you can save travel time by conducting meetings on the Web by using chat software, such as Microsoft NetMeeting, or Mirabilis's ICQ. The meeting participants can share files, and they can make notes on virtual whiteboards. If you have an inexpensive PC video camera ($299) you conduct more personal meetings via videoconferencing, where the participants can see and speak to each other. There's no time or money wasted in plane travel. Obviously, for initial meetings with new clients, you'll want to meet them face to face. But you may be like Kay Royce, who runs a national security firm with subcontractors in each state in Australia. Kay has never met many of the company's clients, and although she tries to meet subcontractors, she says: 'There are people with our company I've never met face to face, although I communicate regularly with them by phone, e-mail and fax.'

Kay believes that her company could not have grown as rapidly as it has without the Internet:

> Easy communication has made our growth possible. For example, we do all our company training from our Web site. New subcontractors can watch presentations directly on the site, and if they have questions they can type them into a form, and the forms are e-mailed directly to the person who handles training.

The Internet lets you save on premises and staff

What could you do if you could save the monthly lease on your business premises—and not simply the lease, but the other costs associated with it, such as electricity?

One of the major ways to save money is by using the Internet to turn either part or all of your business into a 'virtual' organisation—an organisation which exists almost completely in cyberspace. In fact, if you're in an industry such as financial services, or information brokering, there's no need for you to have a physical office at all. Your business can exist completely in cyberspace. Your staff can work from home, and they can communicate with clients and with colleagues via e-mail and through your Web site. The benefits of this are that you free yourself from the costs of buying or leasing business premises.

The virtual organisation business model works for many kinds of businesses. Jerry Fine of Thaddeus Books created an electronic bookstore. He sells antiquarian and out-of-print books through the Web site that is his electronic shopfront. All sales are made via e-mail or fax.

Saving on other costs

The Internet can save you money on many other costs. For example, on advertising, and on market research. Advertising costs can cripple a small business, especially in the early years, and it's almost impossible to get a small business up and running without spending money on a Yellow Pages ad. Although the Internet doesn't completely replace Yellow Pages advertising, you can get a listing in many online directories for free. You can also gain free advertising on other business's Web sites, via banner exchange programs.

How much is your business spending on advertising? As well as your Yellow Pages advertising, perhaps you advertise in your local paper, or on radio or on television. No matter how you spend your advertising dollars, you know:

- Advertising is expensive.
- To be effective, you need to advertise consistently.
- At least half of your advertising is a complete waste of time—but which half?

You may still need to advertise in other media, but the Internet can cut down on the amount of advertising you need to do.

Many small businesses never bother with market research. This means that they produce products and services, and then pray that they'll be able to sell them. This is inefficient, and it's also a highway to the bankruptcy courts. If you know what your customers' needs are, you can create products which will meet those needs: you have an instant market. On the Internet, most of our market research is completely free, and being able to conduct sensible market research can save you creating products that no one wants to buy.

IS YOUR BUSINESS SUITABLE FOR THE INTERNET ENVIRONMENT?

Not all businesses can go global. Some businesses are local in scope. If, for example, you run a service business in your local area, such as a garden maintenance service, you won't be looking for new clients in Singapore or Chicago. However, by joining the global Internet community, you will garner information which will help you to run your business more efficiently. For example, if you run a garden maintenance service, the Internet gives you instant access to unlimited information on horticulture. If you aren't sure of how to handle a particular plant, the National Botanic Gardens (URL: http://155.187.10.12/anbg) would be sure to have the information you need. The Internet could also help you to value add to your business—you could offer a free horticultural consultancy service to your clients.

Plus, if you want to expand your business, you can locate investors. Clifford Martinson found investors for his home renovation company in a Usenet newsgroup. Clifford posted to the newsgroup on an almost daily basis, providing answers to questions like: 'I've got two big cracks in our foundation, and it's causing problems—what can I do?' and 'What's the best flooring for our kitchen?' He became a popular personality on the newsgroup, and this led to his meeting Australian regulars offline—several of these people invested in his business, and one became his new partner: 'The weirdest thing is, my new partner lives a few suburbs away from me. You think of the Internet putting you in touch with people on the other side of the world, but it also gets you local contacts.'

Perhaps you have objections to the brave new virtual world. If so, please take the time to think your objections through. Perhaps they're not so much objections, as wariness of something new. The Internet won't change your business in any basic way, but if your business ideas are sound, it will help you to increase your business and to make more money painlessly. If you've been struggling with your business, your online contacts can help you.

If you're uncertain about the Internet

If you're still not sure about the Internet, consider that:

- **Global business is for you even if you're a technophobe.**
  Current technology takes the 'compute' out of 'computer'—think
  of your new PC as a cross between a video phone, a fax, a TV,
  a radio, and a VCR . . . and much, much more. However, you
  still need to do the work. All the technology in the world is no
  substitute for your energy, enthusiasm and enterprise.
- **Global business is for you if your small business is going
  through rough times.** If all your customers have blown away
  with the wind, you either need to get into a new business, or you
  need to find new prospects. No matter what you want to sell,
  there are people who will buy. With an online connection, your
  potential customers number in the millions.
- **Global business is for you if you don't yet have a small
  business, but would like to.** If you want to be your own boss,
  but aren't sure what kind of business is right for you, you can
  develop your own niche. The Internet makes it possible to mine
  the smallest niches, and to make them pay.
- **Global business is for you if you have an idea for a niche
  product or service.** If, for example, you want to turn your hobby
  of collecting cigarette cards of the 1940s into a business, the
  Internet may be the only way to do it profitably.
- **Global business is for you if you realise that your competitors are using the new technology.** When your competitors
  are using the Internet, they're spending less money. This means
  that they're able to invest more money into their businesses—
  which will grow, perhaps at your expense.

So, what is the Internet, how do you get on it, how much time
does it take to set up your connection and get your business out
there—and how will it make a difference to your business? This book
will show you how to start using the Internet to make your SOHO
business grow.

HOW TO USE THIS BOOK

If you don't already have an online connection, then make getting
one your first step. The Internet is only a tool, how you use it depends

on what you want to do. Initially, don't worry about getting your business online; just get connected and familiarise yourself with e-mail and the World Wide Web. Start to use these tools in your business. You'll find information on hardware and software in Appendix I, and a list of Internet Service Providers right around Australia in the back of the book.

Next, as you read the book, think about developing a Web site for your business, and work out what you want the site to do for you. Of course, you want the site to make money, but you also need to know what you're selling, how you'll present your products on the site, how you'll get customers to your site, and how you'll take orders and ship them.

As soon as you have a clear idea of what you want your site to do for your business, work out how much you want to spend on the site. As you'll see, it's possible to do this inexpensively. You can create a Web site yourself, and have an Internet presence for around $40 a month.

Then go ahead and create your site. Don't worry about making it perfect. You can make changes as you discover what your customers want from your site, and how they actually use it. You may get a few surprises here: your customers may want help and information you haven't anticipated.

You'll find lots of examples in the book of how people are using the Internet inexpensively and simply to develop their businesses, and you can too. Good luck!

chapter 1

Going online

In this chapter we cover some Internet basics, such as arranging your all-important online connection via an Internet Services Provider. We also learn about POP (Post Office Protocol) e-mail accounts, and why they're vital. We go into some detail about e-mail, because e-mail is fundamental to your business now and in the future. Then we introduce you to the World Wide Web, discovering search engines and how to use them. Finally we'll think about creating your own Web site—do you really need one and, if you do, why?

INTERNET SERVICE PROVIDERS

You gain access to the Internet through companies called Internet Service Providers or large companies called online services. Most small businesses need an ISP. This is because the online services such as CompuServe and America Online, while excellent for individuals, are too slow and expensive for efficient business use. The next step, then, is to contact an Internet Service Provider. You hook your computer up to their computers, and you then have access to the Internet.

There are hundreds of ISPs. They range from small companies providing access to a couple of hundred people on a community basis, to large companies providing access to many thousands of people Australia-wide. You'll find a list of many providers, in all areas of Australia, in the back of this book. To find others, perhaps closer to you, look up 'Internet' in the Yellow Pages. You can usually sign up with an ISP over the phone. Some have specialty software packages which help you to get online simply by installing the programs; these packages are usually free.

When you sign up, you'll be given a user name, and a password to access the service. You'll also be given some instructions on phone numbers to dial into, and how to enter the information such as the provider's domain name (Net address) into your computer's software. It's a good idea to have information like the kind of computer and modem you have, and what software you're running on the machine, handy when you call your ISP to obtain your connection. When you've done that, plug your modem into your phone line, and press the Connect button. You're online.

Choosing the right ISP

Although finding an ISP and gaining Internet access is easy, finding the *right* ISP for your business is more difficult. When you use an ISP for home and hobby access to the Internet, you have minimal requirements. Although it may be annoying to receive busy signals when you try to connect, it won't hit your wallet. Using the Internet for your business, however, means that you want a service which is reliable. When you dial in, you want to be able to get online immediately, you want to be able to send and receive your e-mail, and you want to be able to make checks on your Web site.

To start out with the correct mindset to find the right ISP for your business, you should know that there are many providers, both large and small. These providers offer a range of services, but unfortunately price is no guide to the quality of the service.

Here's how to find the right provider for your business:

1. Work out a budget, and decide how much you want to spend on your online activities. If you're not sure what the Internet can do for your business, then make the budget a minimal one—say $50 a month. Don't forget to include the cost of toll phone calls, if this is an issue. Many providers offer almost unlimited access for around $30–$40 a month.
2. Compare. Ask around: how much are your colleagues, competitors and customers paying for Internet access? What are they getting for their money?

3. Try out the freebies. Some ISPs (OzEmail, Telstra Big Pond) offer one month's free access to let you try out their service. Try several. When you're trying out a service, give it a good workout. Use it as often as you can, at various times of the day and night. Once you get used to using the Internet for business, you may want to change your overseas calls to Internet conferences. Take note of the provider's busy times, and also whether you can access a Help number after hours.

4. When you've narrowed the search down to around two or three contenders, look at the plans they offer closely. Basic plans offer either unlimited access for a flat fee, or charge an hourly rate, with cheaper rates at 'night owl' times of the night. Aside from the access/payment plan, consider the area the provider covers. If you do business only in your local area or state, then a local provider will suit you. However, if you travel overseas on business, you'll need a national provider with international local-call dial-up numbers in the countries to which you travel. When you have this option, you can use your Internet account no matter where you are—no need to change any of the settings on your computer; only the dial-up number will change. Be sure to ask whether there is an additional charge when you use the provider's international 'roaming' options.

5. Check what you get for your money. All ISPs will offer you space on their servers to set up your own Web site, but do ask how much space you're allocated. Five megs would be a reasonable amount to begin with. You should make sure that if you want to set up a site which needs 50 megs of space next year, that this won't be a problem—and that you won't be charged excessively for the extra space. (Note: if you intend using a database, or a lot of graphics on your site, you'll go over five megs very quickly.)

6. Ask the provider whether you're allowed more than one e-mail address per account. How many? What are the charges for additional e-mail addresses? When you get your business online, you'll want each of your staff to have their own e-mail address. Adding e-mail addresses becomes an issue because each address takes up a 'mailbox' on the provider's servers. The usual amount of space allocated to a mailbox is around one meg, which is not a huge amount. If you're in the graphic design business, for example, you'll fill up a one meg mailbox very quickly.

7. Ask the provider whether you can use your own browser and e-mail application. Some providers include a browser and e-mail application with the service, which you're obliged to use. This is often a non-standard application developed or purchased by the provider. Sometimes these proprietary applications have bugs that are revealed only when you start to use them. You may also have problems integrating the proprietary browser and e-mail applications with your other applications.

8. Ask the provider whether a premium is charged for high-speed modem access.

9. If you intend developing your own home page or Web site, you should also ask what services are provided to help you with this. Does the provider offer a wizard (an automated application) to guide you through the construction of your Web page? Although an automated application only creates a 'bare bones' site, it does give you a foundation to build on.

A POP e-mail account

It's vital that you choose an access provider who will furnish you with a POP e-mail account. POP (Post Office Protocol) is the standard e-mail system used on the Internet. With a POP account, you'll be able to contact anyone who has Internet access, and they'll be able to contact you. All ISPs provide you with POP accounts, whereas online services do not. Online services such as America Online and Compu-Serve have their own e-mail systems, and these were created before Internet access was important.

What's the big deal about a POP account? A POP account is much more flexible than a non-POP account. You'll want your own domain name—maybe even several domains, if you have several products for which you're trying to develop a brand name—and a POP account lets you create as many e-mail addresses at as many domains as you need. For example, my domain name is www.angelabooth.com.au. Since I have a POP account, and my own domain name, I can create as many e-mail accounts as I need: sales@angelabooth.com.au, info@angelabooth.com.au, accounts@angelabooth.com.au, etc. A POP account allows you to create mailboxes for all your employees.

In addition, with a POP account you can use whichever e-mail software you please. I use Microsoft Outlook 98, but other excellent e-mail programs include Pegasus Mail and Eudora Pro Mail. There are many others. If you don't have a POP account, you're forced to use the online service's proprietary software, which has fewer options.

E-MAIL

What's so great about e-mail?

E-mail is electronic mail. The easiest way to think of how it works is to remember the classroom. If you wanted to get a note to a kid on the other side of the room, you nudged the person next to you, whispered the name of the addressee, and handed over the note. Within a minute or two, the note arrived at its destination. E-mail works the same way. You type a message in your e-mail program, address the message, usually by clicking on a name in your program's Address Book, and press the Send button. Your computer passes the message to your ISP's

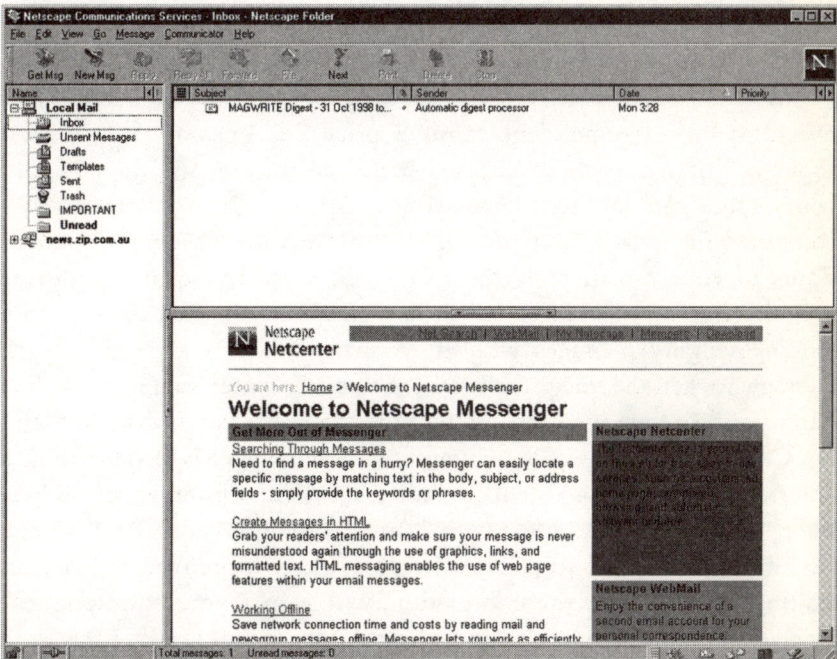

The Netscape Communicator e-mail client: e-mail is a feature of most Web browsers.

computer, then the message is passed on from computer to computer across the Internet until it reaches its destination.

The beauty of e-mail is that it's both the fastest and the easiest—as well as the cheapest—way to communicate. Most messages you send arrive at their destination within a few minutes, often within a couple of seconds. You can log onto your ISP anytime, wherever you are, and send messages, or download (jargon for collect) messages which have been sent to you. When you click on the Reply button to a message, the address of the sender and the subject are already filled in. Type your answer, and press Send, and your answer wings its way to your correspondent within seconds—even if they're on the other side of the world.

E-mail is faster than fax, and more efficient than a phone call, in the sense that e-mail gives you a record of your interaction with an individual, or with a company, and it eliminates telephone tag. You will also find that because of its perceived informality, and ease of use, you get a fast response. Indeed, you'll get responses from people who ignore letters and won't take phone calls. The speed of e-mail has contributed to it becoming the preferred communication method in large companies in the United States, and Australia is not far behind.

Most messages you receive can be answered within a minute or two. If your correspondent wants a price-list, or more information about a product, you can cut and paste the information directly into your reply from another file on your computer. Or, you can attach a computer file which contains all the information the correspondent wants to your e-mail reply. You may also want to attach a photo or a multimedia presentation to an e-mail message. However, before sending lengthy messages with attachments you should send a quick message to get the recipient's OK to send the file; some networked systems refuse long messages because they're not set up to handle them.

Consider how much faster (and cheaper) e-mail is than writing a letter to your correspondent, printing the letter, printing an address label, and putting the letter with printed brochures into an envelope which you then need to take to the post office. Moreover, rather than waiting a few days for the information, with e-mail your correspondent receives the information within a few seconds of you pressing the Send button on your computer. By using e-mail to respond to customer inquiries, you'll make big savings in time and in expenses.

You won't want to entirely eliminate the print brochures and flyers you send out by postal mail; not everyone has e-mail, after all, and even people who use e-mail and feel comfortable with it may prefer to shop in more conventional ways. However, the customers who find you through your Web site will usually prefer to deal with you via e-mail, simply because it's faster. For example, I love buying goods on the Internet, even if I'm paying by cheque rather than using an online transaction facility. I can copy and paste the vendor's name and address into my chequebook program, and I can have my printer zip out an addressed envelope within a few seconds.

What will you use e-mail for?

You'll mainly use e-mail for straight communications, in exactly the same way that you use letters and your phone and fax. However, there are many other ways in which you can use e-mail—as a promotional tool, for example, or to handle customer queries.

You can also use e-mail to build up your own tailored marketing list of people who are interested in your product. To do this, begin collecting the addresses of the people you communicate with. You may want to make different e-mail contact lists; you can

Sending e-mail to groups of people

It's important to understand the 'group-mail' features of your e-mail software, and how they work. Group e-mail lets you send the same e-mail message to several (or many) recipients at the same time. For example, most e-mail programs let you send e-mail to a complete address book, or a distribution list, on your computer. When sending e-mail to groups, use the Bcc: line. 'Bcc' means 'Blind carbon copy'; it ensures that everyone on the list will get a copy of the message, but they won't see the e-mail addresses of everyone else who got a copy. Some e-mail programs won't allow you to have an address in the Bcc: line alone; they insist that you have an address in the To: line. The easy way around this is to put your own e-mail address in the To: line, and then put the distribution list's name on the Bcc: line.

Why not put the distribution list in the To: line? If you put the list's name in the To: line, everyone who receives the list will also receive the names of all the other recipients in the header of the message. This isn't a disaster if it's a small group, but it will annoy recipients if you have thousands of names in the group and they have to scroll past all the names to get to the message. You may also want the people receiving the message to think it's a personal message to them, or perhaps you want to keep your distribution list a secret.

have lists of your current customers, potential customers (people who've inquired about your product), suppliers, and so on. When you add people to a group, you can send a single message that will reach every person in that group's list.

The following are common uses for e-mail:

- Distributing newsletters and other information—on the Internet, newsletters are often used as a promotional tool, just as they are in the real world.
- To announce new products and services.
- To announce price changes and specials.
- To conduct market research and to ask for feedback on your products.

You can use e-mail in any way which makes sense to you. However, don't overdo the e-mail contact. You wouldn't call someone several times a week, nor would you send them a fax or letter that often. E-mail is cheap and easy, but use restraint. Make sure that when you send a message it's information that the recipient needs.

Using your e-mail productively

The key to using e-mail productively is to make it easy for your correspondents to read and to answer your messages. Remember that people log onto the Internet using many different kinds of computers and software; you have no way of knowing whether the recipient of your 280K message logged on using a powerful desktop machine, or whether they logged on using a tiny hand-held machine. Therefore you should always send plain text messages, unless you've discussed what computers and software your recipients are using. If you intend sending large files over the Internet, send a warning message first.

It's also annoying to receive a file and not be able to view the contents. For example, if you want to send a proposal to a contact, first send a message asking what format they would like the proposal in; should you send it as plain text, or as a Microsoft Powerpoint multimedia presentation? They may reply that you should send the plain text, and ask you to copy the full presentation onto a disk and send that via ordinary mail, so that the large file doesn't overwhelm their e-mail message box.

E-mail faux pas

Unsolicited e-mail is called 'spam', and Internet users hate it. On the face of it, this seems a superb concept. You can create your promotional message, and send it out to thousands—hundreds of thousands—at next to no cost. You don't even need to buy a mailing list. Software exists which will winnow e-mail addresses from Usenet and ISPs, and automatically send these people your message. Great idea, eh? No, it's a rotten idea.

Do not send unsolicited e-mail, to anyone, ever, for any reason. If you decide to go ahead and do it anyway, because visions of dollars are dancing in your head, be prepared to lose your reputation, your business, and perhaps your sanity in the process. Internet users retaliate to spam, often in ways that seem out of proportion to the offence. For example, if your ISP is sent a twelve gigabyte file of garbage, as a retaliation for your spam, it will crash your ISP's servers. When your ISP learns that the garbage file was directed to them because you sent out spam, you will lose your account. You may even be sued. A Texas spammer was successfully sued in November 1997; $50 000 in damages was awarded to the ISP involved.

In the physical world, if you send out a batch of a few thousand letters in a direct mail campaign, you bear the cost. Content aside, you pay for the paper and the stamps. The only cost to the consumers is the time it takes to glance at your letter, and to either discard it or act on it. The online world is different. The costs of distributing advertising messages is borne by both the advertiser and the consumers. Every consumer pays a fee to receive information via the Internet. Some pay by the hour, some pay per message, but everyone pays in some way. If you're wondering why Internet users get so steamed about spam, ask yourself whether you would accept collect phone calls from telemarketers, or whether you would pay the postage due on the advertising letters that you receive in the mail.

THE WORLD WIDE WEB

The World Wide Web is a subset of the Internet. Basically, the Web consists of a network of interlinked documents, which work together using an Internet protocol called HTML (HyperText Markup Language). In a sense, there is no Web apart from the Internet, because the Internet is the information transfer system without which the Web would not exist.

The interlinked documents, or 'pages', which make up the Web, are usually combined into Web sites—that is, a group of pages on a computer which is owned by a company, institution or person. You can access the pages on the computer where they're stored, no matter where the computer is in the world, because they're written in HTML, which tells your Web browser (the program you're using to access the Web) how to display the pages, along with their various elements, such as graphics and forms, on the site.

Creating a Web site is as easy as creating documents using your word processor, thanks to the many Web-authoring programs on the market. You don't have to learn to write computer code.

Exploring the Web

The first thing you should do when you get online is to find other businesses in your area, either geographically or in your area of interest. You may be as lucky as Ann Zustak of the What's in a Name company, and find that you're the only one offering your product online—or the first to offer your product. Ann offers gifts, such as wall plaques which give the history of a person's name. If you're not the first or the only company offering a specific product, you'll want to see what others are offering to give you ideas for your own business's transition to online trading.

You can locate businesses similar to yours using the search engines of the World Wide Web. With millions of computers connected to the Internet, finding a specific Web site could be a nightmare. However, the Web provides software running on superfast computers which allows you to find anyone or any business online reasonably quickly. These are known as search engines, and you'll soon become familiar with them. The Web search engines simplify the Web.

When you're looking for information on the Web, rather than company or personal home pages, you'll see that there are three main kinds of Web sites which provide information:

1. Primary information sites: these are sites which store actual information. They include texts, library catalogues, databases of electronic newspapers and magazines, and so on.
2. Primary link sites: these are sites which carry pointers to primary

information sites. For example, BUBL at http://bubl.ac.uk is a good primary link site.

3. Simple link sites: these are sites that carry a selection of links to other sites. And from those sites, you'll find links to yet more sites . . . and so on. Many personal and company Web sites carry links.

USING SEARCH ENGINES

Search engines come in two varieties: subject guides, such as Yahoo!, and keyword searchers, such as InfoSeek. Subject guides are good for overviews on a topic, while the keyword searchers take you to specific, focused information. Search Insider http://www.searchinsider.com provides good information on using Web search engines, as well as updates on the capabilities of the various engines. New features and capabilities are being added all the time, and when you use the Web to hunt for information, you'll want to stay abreast of these changes.

A selection of subject guides

The WWW Virtual Library

URL: http://www.w3.org/pub/DataSources/bySubject/Overview.html
One of the oldest of the subject guides on the Web. The WWW Library category editors are experts in their particular field, and you'll find that it's a good jumping off point for further exploration.

Internet Resources Meta-Index

URL: http://www.ncsa.uiuc.edu/SDG/Software/Mosaic/MetaIndex. html
Consider this a resource to other resources, rather than a true subject guide. It directs you to guides, directories and indices all over the World Wide Web.

Yahoo!

URL: www.yahoo.com
Yahoo is an enormous collection of Web links, which are arranged in an hierarchical tree. It's a subject guide, but it also incorporates a search engine. You'll find the Australian Yahoo at www.yahoo.com.au; try it first for Australian information.

Hassle-free Internet searching

Finding information on the World Wide Web is simple. Most searches are basic. You enter your query terms (what you're looking for) into a search engine's query box, press the Search button, and within a few seconds—hey presto—you have the information. Most of the Internet searches you conduct will probably be of this variety. Unfortunately, problems can arise. This basic-search technique works best if you're looking for something very specific. It's not useful on generic-type searches, such as for 'books', 'software', etc. When you're doing generic searches, you'll end up with results in the millions unless you add focus to your search by adding more search terms. At this stage, you should use the search engine's Power search features, so that you can add your additional terms in a way that's acceptable to that particular search engine facility.

Here's how to do a simple search. Let's say that you remember reading about an Australian shareware program which allowed you to track your stocks in real time, and could interface with your accounting program. Luckily, you remember the name of the program: Streepwood Stock Magnet. You use Australian Yahoo, at www.yahoo.com.au, enter 'Streepwood Stock Magnet' into the query box, and you have a link to the program's home page within a second or so.

Currently my favourite search engines for simple searches are Northern Light at http://www.northernlight.com which finds information world-wide, and Web Wombat at http://www2.webwombat.com.au, to find information on sites within Australia.

Let's see how this process works in more detail. You own a gift shop. Greeting cards are very popular, and you hope to locate some new suppliers. You decide that a Web search will be the fastest way. You decide to start with Web Wombat. In the query box on the Web Wombat search page, type: 'greeting cards'.

Go on, try it.

I did, and got the following result:

GREETING (273)

CARD(4055) CARD1(3) CARDION(1) CARD1WIN(1) CARD2(2) CARD2ON(1) CARD2WIN(1) CARD3(1) CARD336(1) CARD3ON(1) CARD4ON(1) CARD5ON(1) CARD6ON(1) CARD7ON(1) CARD8ON(1) CARDAK(6) CARDALL(2) CARDAMOM(4) CARDAMON(2) CARDANO(4) CARDASSIAN(2) CARDASSIANS(1) etc. etc. etc.

CARDS(2786)

Overwhelming? Not really. I found three likely looking prospects out of the ten hits on the first page.

You, as the gift shop owner, could have clicked on these three links and viewed the Web sites. If the sites didn't look as if the company produced the cards you wanted, you could have looked at the next couple of pages of Web Wombat's returns to your query. Within less than ten minutes, you could have sent e-mail to a few prospects, or picked up the phone and given them a call.

This is Australia

URL: http://springboard.telstra.com.au/index.html
Telstra's guide to Australian sites, as well as overseas ones. Consider it a good resource to Australian government and legal information, as well as to commercial sites.

The WebWombat search engine: one of several excellent Australian search engines on the Web.

A selection of keyword searchers

InfoSeek

URL: www.infoseek.com

InfoSeek is one of the most popular search engines. It's useful because it allows you to be very specific in your searches. You can search for fields in Web sites, such as titles, hyperlinks and URLs, plus use case-sensitive searches. It also provides a number of tools, each with a specific purpose. These include classifieds, a chat area, maps—including maps of Australian locations from MapQuest. In addition, in partnership with Disney, InfoSeek launched *GO Network* (URL: www.GO.com), a Web portal designed to give users faster access to the information they need in both their home and working lives. As with all of the most popular search engines, InfoSeek is constantly adding new services.

AltaVista

URL: http:www.altavista.com

AltaVista is very fast, and it can handle millions of search requests at any one time, so your search request is hardly ever refused. Alta Vista has the largest full-text database index of any of the Web search engines, and is updated once a week.

Excite

URL: www.excite.com

Excite has a number of services you'll find useful in your business, including company and stock tracking. You can also build your own entrance page to Excite, so that you only see the information you want to see whenever you access the site.

In many cases, you won't even need a search engine to find a company online. Let's say you use Corel software, and you want to find Corel. Companies like to use their trademarked name as their Internet address, so you'd guess that you might find Corel at www.corel.com, and you'd be right.

CREATING YOUR OWN WEB SITE

All businesses need a Web site. Your Web site may be as simple as a single page which gives your contact details, or it may be many thousands of pages long, and have the capacity to perform electronic commerce transactions.

Let's look at two scenarios. Robert Samuals owns a hair-dressing salon in a Sydney suburb. Robert isn't sure whether he needs a Web site. He doubts it. After all, his clients are either long-time clients who've been coming to the salon for years, or they're passing traffic, enticed into the shop by special offers.

Colleen Ryan owns Paper-Aware, a specialty stationery supply business. Colleen offers hundreds of different varieties of paper, all made from recycled material. Colleen has a warehouse in Melbourne. She wants a Web site. Many of her papers are unique, and she wants to offer them to a wider clientele than she can reach with an ad in the Yellow Pages.

> **A handy list of keyword search engines**
>
> *AltaVista:* http://www.AltaVista.digital.com
> *Beaucoup:* http://www.beaucoup.com
> *DejaNews:* (searches Usenet) http://www.dejanews.com
> *Excite:* http://www.excite.com
> *HotBot:* http://www.hotbot.com
> *I-Explorer:* http://www.i-explorer.com
> *InfoSeek:* http://www.infoseek.com
> *Intuitive Web Index:* http://intuitive.iexp.com
> *Link Monster:* http://www.linkmonster.com
> *Lycos:* http://www.lycos.com
> *Magellan:* http://www.mckinley.com
> *Pathfinder:* http://www.pathfinder.com
> *Switchboard:* (US phone numbers) http://www.switchboard.com
> *Web Crawler:* http://www.webcrawler.com
> *WWWWorm:* http://guano.cs.colorado.edu/wwww/
> *Yahoo:* http://www.yahoo.com

Let's look at some of the reasons for creating a Web site, and then we'll decide whether Robert and Colleen would benefit from a site, and how.

Reasons for creating a Web site

- To win new customers.
- To promote your products, which you sell in retail outlets or by mail order.
- To take orders and appointments online.
- To distribute information about your company and products.
- To give better customer service and support.

- To develop relationships which may lead to new customers.
- To develop a better relationship with your current customers.
- To provide an internal communications system for your company.
- To give information to shareholders and encourage their support.
- To sell advertising space on your site.

Winning new customers

This is a good reason to create a Web site. However, winning any customer costs your business. You will need to devote time and energy to promoting the site so that you attract visitors to it, and you will have to spend time and energy turning your online prospects into customers. How much time and expense does it take for you to get a customer using traditional methods—that is, via advertising, direct mail, and so on? Work out how much each customer you win using traditional ways costs you. When you have calculated this figure, you can work out how much you're willing to spend on developing a Web site, and on the ongoing promotions of the site.

Promoting your products

Selling products online is not for everyone, however you can still use the Internet as a promotional facility. Let's say you own a small business in any Australian suburb. Your promotional efforts are directed to the local community, and you target your customers via ads in your local paper and mailbox drops. You might think the Internet is not for you—but you'd be wrong. Tammy Keyes owns Feline and Pooch Shampoo, a cat and dog grooming business. She used to spend $60 a week advertising in the local paper. She says: 'Some weeks I wouldn't get a single call. But over a couple of months since putting up my Web site, I've gained twenty new customers—that's repeat customers, people who've booked monthly grooming services for their dog.' Tammy saves the $200+ a month the ads in the local paper cost and, since her Web site costs nothing except her Internet access of $39 paid to her ISP each month, she's very excited about the potential of the site. 'I have a contact in Queensland who makes up botanical shampoos and flea rinses for pets. I've started advertising the products on the Web site, and get around five inquiries a day. This past week, I've made $300 selling products. Now I'm looking for other products

I can sell via the site.' Tammy is successfully expanding her local business, by promoting it online.

Taking orders and appointments online

You can take orders online in several ways. The easiest way is just to have customers contact you via e-mail. You send them vital ordering information, such as the price (in US dollars for overseas sales), and payment and delivery options. Payment may be via cheque, credit card, or electronic payment to your bank account. For products weighing a couple of kilos or less, you could send them via FedEx or DHL; have the current charges ready to send to customers.

It's slightly more complex to take orders and payments directly online, but it pays off in efficiency by ensuring that the customer provides you with all the information you need to complete the order, such as full product details, credit card information, plus their mailing address. As a bonus, this information is already in electronic format— no need to type or scan it into your system. You have two choices: a Web-based form, or a 'shopping cart' system.

You can create simple forms using your Web authoring program's scripting system. When the customer fills in the form, the order is sent to you via e-mail. If you're selling more than three or four products, consider using a shopping cart system. This is simply a series of Web forms which customers can use to place orders. Customers browse the site's product catalogue, making selections as they do so. When they've finished shopping, they go to the 'checkout', which gives them the total of the order, and asks them for credit card number and shipping details.

Distributing information about your company and products

A Web site is a great way to cut printing and distribution costs. Why not let your Web site visitors use their printers to print out the information they want? They get only the information they need, and it's available when they want it. The *Trading Post* is a well known offline, and now online, classified advertising newspaper. Bill Nolan, the *Trading Post*'s General Manager of Marketing and Advertising, says that people are using the online version of the newspaper to find cars they want: a man from Dubbo arrived at a Sydney address to look at a car he wanted to buy clutching a piece of A4 paper on which he'd printed out the car's details and image. The *Trading Post* has started an Internet division of the company, to deal solely with online sales.

What sort of information could you put on your site? Basically, anything you think visitors would want to know about you:

* your product catalogue;
* contact information;
* a Frequently Asked Questions (FAQ) page;
* job vacancies;
* after-sales service information; and
* specials and news about new products.

Although you won't make money directly by putting this data on your Web site, you will be operating your business more efficiently. Online information makes it easier for potential clients to find out more about you, and for clients to get what they want from you. Phone calls cost you money, even if you have voice-mail. How many clients are you losing because prospects don't want to spend precious minutes navigating your voice-mail system? A recent survey by Ernst and Young of the executives at a human resources conference in the US showed that e-mail had taken over from the phone as the primary means of business communication.

Giving better customer service and support

Customer service is a major cost for many companies. If this is your problem, are you losing repeat sales because your customers are dissatisfied with the service they were given?

An Adelaide car dealership is adding its service and repair shop to their Web site. The City Holden site at http://www.city holden.com.au has been online since the start of 1998. James Newton, who created the site, says: 'Vehicle servicing is a vital part of the dealership, and we're adding a facility where clients will be able to book their cars in for service at a time to suit them, even over the weekend. This also means that clients will have a complete record of work that has been done on their vehicle, and they can refer to it at any time.'

Developing relationships which may lead to new customers

Don't think of your Web site as static—as the online version of a Yellow Pages ad. Your Web site is all about interaction; be prepared to 'meet' the people who visit the site. Give them a reason to communicate with you, so that you can begin to form a relationship. You know what it takes to create relationships in the 'real' world; think of your relationships on the Web in the same way. First, collect e-mail addresses. You can do this by offering a giveaway, a free newsletter, or other item. Then, use the addresses. Notify your distribution list when you have a new product or service which may interest them.

Developing a better relationship with your current customers

The Internet offers a way for you to learn more about your current customers. What do they like about your products? What do they dislike? This information is invaluable—it can save you making costly mistakes. In return for the information, give your customers a reward, such as a discount on another product.

Providing an internal communications system for your company

If you have branch offices, a simple way to create an internal, Web-based communications system is to create a private Web site, which can only be accessed by the people in your company. You can do this cheaply, by using a product like Microsoft FrontPage, a Web site creation product. Your employees can access your site from anywhere in the world, as long as they have a computer and a phone line. They can access the company database, share files, send messages, and even conduct virtual meetings.

Giving information to shareholders

If your company has shareholders, you can set up a Web site for them. As well as offering information about your company, such as the latest share prices, it can contain special offers for shareholders, company news, special reports about your industry, and more.

Selling advertising space on your site

It's easy enough to set up a Web site—why would anyone want to advertise on yours? If you can write a letter, you can create a Web site, but not everyone has the time or the inclination. A week after Tammy Keyes's Feline and Pooch Shampoo went online, a local vet placed an ad on her site, and she had an inquiry about a boarding kennel which wanted to do the same. The vet took boarders too, and he didn't want a competitor, so Tammy refused the kennel.

What about Robert and Colleen? How will they be able to benefit from using the Internet for their businesses?

Hairdressing salon owner Robert has been talking to his suppliers. His major suppliers are developing an Internet order-fulfilment program, and salons which place orders via the Internet will get discounts on all products ordered online. Robert is pleased that not only will he save money, but the Internet ordering system will also save time: he can place orders whenever he pleases, rather than once a month when the supplier's representative is in the area. While Robert won't need a Web site to place orders with his suppliers, he likes the idea that he can use his Web site to promote special offers and new products, so he's decided to develop a small site.

Colleen's commissioned a Web designer to create an e-commerce-enabled site for her stationery supply company, PaperAware. Although the site she has in mind will cost around $10 000, she is sure that she will get an excellent return on her investment within the first year. She's already using her e-mail to do some networking online, and two US companies are interested in distributing her products there. Colleen is working out a budget, and is developing an online marketing plan to promote her site. She intends to use her site to win new customers, and to sell and promote her products worldwide.

If you're in business, you need a Web site. Your chief reason for developing one, even if it's only a tiny site of one page, will be so people can *find you*. Look at the Web as a global, interactive form of the Yellow Pages, and your Web site is your own entry in this system. It allows your customers to locate you, even if they can't remember your name—they may only remember your location and what you sell.

The best part is that developing and maintaining a site can be very inexpensive. You can create the site in an hour or two, and your site can be hosted for around $10 a month.

If you're convinced that your business needs a Web site, we'll discuss creating a site in the next chapter.

chapter 2

Planning and creating your business's Web site

Let's dig in and get our hands dirty as we plan your Web site. We'll look at how others have created effective Web sites, and find out how they did it. We'll learn what they considered important, why you need to think about how the Internet will impact on your business as a whole, and what resources you'll allocate to the project. Will you hire a designer or will you design your site yourself? The answer depends on the time you have, and the funds—we'll look at both options. Finally, we'll think about who you'll choose to host your site.

PLANNING YOUR SITE: IMAGE, TITLE AND MORE

The first step in developing your Web site is to plan it. Planning your Web site takes thought, and time. However, the more carefully you plan, the more successful your site is likely to be. You will also avoid expensive mistakes.

The Web is an excellent place to get help with planning your site. You can find mailing lists (e-mail discussion groups) devoted to site planning, creation, and online sales. Go to the Liszt Mailing List database (www.liszt.com) to find the e-mail addresses for these mailing lists. However, you shouldn't get so caught up in the planning process that you postpone creating your site and putting it online. The Internet changes constantly, and your Web site will always be a work in progress. Of the small business owners I spoke to, many planned their online strategy carefully. Others did no planning at all, they simply put up a basic site, and then began to learn what would work for their business on the Web. Greg Bacia, of Bacia Internet Properties, said: 'Maybe if I'd taken more time to plan, I would have saved time, but I don't think so. The most exciting thing about the Web is that it's so easy to try things. If they don't work, you can try something else.'

Use the first couple of weeks of your Internet connection to investigate some of the possible online options for your business. Your aim may be to extend your business's reach. Perhaps you want to diversify. Or you might want to add extra services, or value-add to the products and services you're selling now. Relax during this exploration period. Talia Grey, of Sareen Arabians, is a professional photographer as well as a breeder of Arabian horses. She feels that the time she spent surfing widely across the Web wasn't wasted. 'I'm glad I took the time to check out other horse breeders' sites. Getting a feel for what works and what doesn't made me more confident that I was making the right choices when it came to planning my Web site.'

Many small business people said they put up their first Web site purely as an experiment. They had no real expectations of how well their business would do. Greg Bacia had just been downsized out of a job. 'I didn't plan the site at all. My wife is a real estate agent, and I developed our site to help her. It was a way for her to keep track of her listings.' In its first few months, he says, the site was visited by no more than one person a week. 'I didn't promote the site at all, so the slow start wasn't surprising.'

Greg was startled when other agents wanted to put their listings onto the site:

> I didn't expect that. They could see the potential before I could. And then it just took off. Now I maintain sites for six other agents. My wife estimates that the Web site helps her make about 30 per cent of her sales. It isn't so much that people see a house on the site, and decide to buy it. What they can do is save time by eliminating houses that are completely unsuitable for them. By the time they make an appointment to see the agent, they've chosen the two or three houses they definitely want to see.

You will change the site as you grow in experience, and also as you learn what kind of an image you want to portray on the Web.

Greg says that six months after he launched his site, he did a complete revamp:

> The original site looked amateurish, and the first page had a large graphic which meant it loaded slowly. I designed a new site which gave us a more professional image. I trimmed all the graphics, and included our logo on each page, and so on. I also had more of an idea of what our target market was, and I designed the new image to appeal to them.

Before you do much else, focus on your site's title. The site's title is important, because that's what will be indexed by search engines. The site's title doesn't need to be your business name. Barry Michael's site, Boots Online, is a perfect example of a business name which also works well as the title for a Web page. Your business name may not be as useful—if your business name is Smith, Jones, Thompson & Associates, it will be almost impossible to find the business's Web site via a search engine, unless it's typed in precisely. This kind of business name also gives no clue as to what kind of business it is. Think of another title for the page; if you're an accountancy firm, for example, call the site *Accountants Central,* for instance. You can then give the business name in the main part of the page.

Talia believes that when you're planning the image you want to portray, you should also give an indicator of your credentials. 'If people have never heard of your business, why should they trust you? I judge Arabian horses at shows all over the world, and I put that on the site.' Putting your credentials online doesn't mean that you have to be famous. If newspaper articles have been written about your business, put those online (with the permission of the copyright holders), or simply put up recommendations from your clients. If any of the clients have a Web site, then link to those sites, and ask them to provide a link to your site.

If at all possible, show examples of your work or products on your Web site. Eileen, of Turtle's Web Art and Design, designs Web sites, so naturally she has a portfolio page of designs she has created for clients. For most businesses, putting your work online is impossible, so do the next best thing: put client referrals online. Keep in mind that the online world is different from the 'real world'. In the real world, your customers can walk into your store, or can visit you in your office. They can see you and the products you sell, or you can tell them about your services. There are many clues to help them to

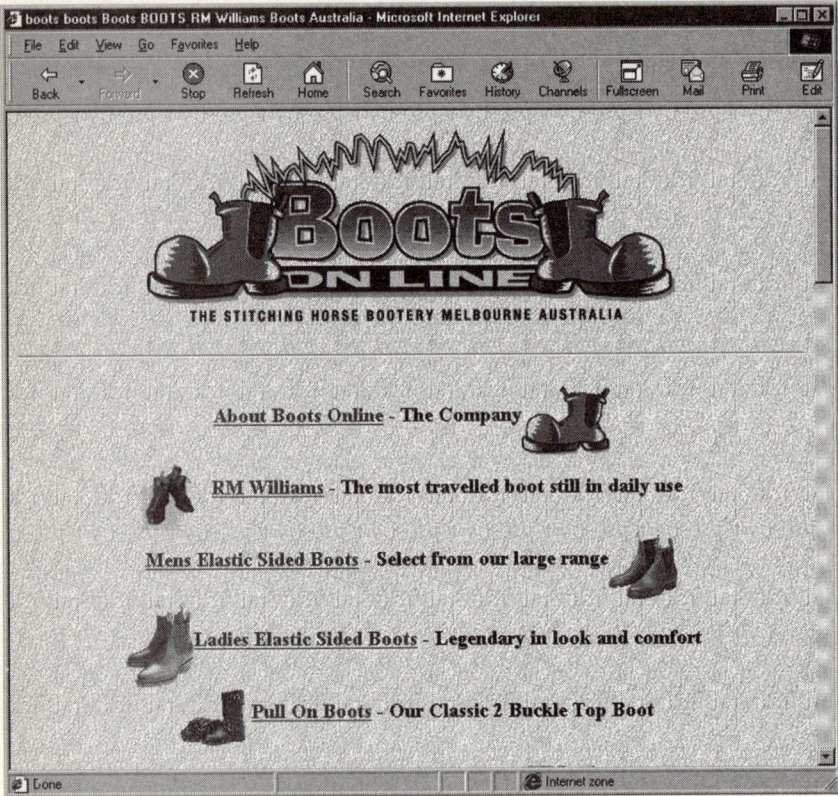

The site's title is also the business name: your Web site's title should be descriptive, so that people can find you in the Web search engines.

learn about you and your business. In the online world, your Web site tells your customers who you are, and what you can do for them. Your Web site has to do a complete selling job on its own. Either showing your work, or demonstrating that many people in the real world use your services, is a way of making you real to the people who will only meet you online.

Talia believes e-mail helps make you real to your online clients. 'When you respond—within hours—to an e-mail message, you become real. Your potential client gets a chance to know you and trust you. Be informal, be brief, but use your e-mail.' She emphasises that responding to e-mail promptly is vital:

When you respond quickly, people can begin to trust you. I check my e-mail every few hours. When I'm away from my office, I have someone else do it for me. My aim is to get a response out to people the same day, within a couple of hours if possible. When people find you online, your Web site is static. A quick response shows them that you're a real person, and that you want to do business with them.

Greg agrees:

Your attitude builds your image. I'm always pleased that people have taken the time to communicate, and I try to show that in my response. If the person e-mailing has left a phone number, I call them or I send a fax. If not, I'll reply by e-mail right away. I know that a prompt response is magic, because that's what people who've bought a property have said.

As you begin to plan your online presence, make some notes about the image you want to portray and what credentials you will put on the site, as well as what content you want to include. The more thought you put into developing a plan for launching your business online, the better prepared you'll be if your venture is even more successful than you hope.

YOU MUST BE COMMITTED TO YOUR SITE'S SUCCESS

When you plan, be realistic. Your site may be instantly successful—if you're offering something that people need, and that they can't get anywhere else. More likely, it will take time to make your site a success. The consensus of opinion of the people I spoke to who were making money online was that you should count on two years for your business to take off online. This means that you need to be committed to your Web site, knowing that it will be a success, if not this year, certainly next year.

Here's a checklist to incorporate into your planning for creating and maintaining a successful Web site:

Have you developed objectives for the site?

1. Is your Web site integrated into your overall business marketing plan?
2. Have you developed procedures for managing the increased communication with customers which will arise from the site? For example: who will manage the e-mail? Do you have information

files developed, which you can send to the people who request them?

3. Have you budgeted time and money for Web site maintenance?

4. Have you budgeted time and money for Web site promotion?

5. Have you decided how you will measure the effectiveness of your site, in line with your objectives?

6. Have you decided how you will change your business strategy in line with the results you achieve? For example, if one of your objectives for the site is to increase the leads for your sales force, do you have a system in place to handle additional leads?

YOUR ONLINE PLANNING GUIDE IN A NUTSHELL

1. Define your business—what image do you want to project online? You can call this your mission statement if you like.

2. Decide what goals you want to achieve with your online presence. What are your objectives? How will your Web site combine with your other business activities?

3. Decide what business resources you'll allocate to your online efforts—create a budget.

4. Decide how large or small your Web site will be. If you choose a small site, your Web site can consist of simply a home page, with some information on who you are, what you do, and how to find you. At the other end of the spectrum, your site could be very sophisticated, with thousands of pages, integrated product ordering, and several database applications. Decide on whether you'll create your site yourself, or whether you will hire someone to create it for you. Doing it yourself is an option if you plan on a simple site. An online catalogue with integrated ordering, however, means that you'll probably need a designer to create the site for you.

5. Set a date for launching your online enterprise.

1. Define your business

It's vital that you define your business in terms of the benefits for your customers. For example, Amy Vansant runs a business called Gourmet Aisle. I first heard about Amy when she sent a message to one of the newsgroups I visit regularly, alt.food.low-fat. The message was brief, simply explaining that Gourmet Aisle sells 4000 different gourmet goodies by the case, for individuals, small stores and caterers. Amy defined her business very clearly in the message: 'Gourmet Aisle means gourmet items by the case.' I admit that I visited the site immediately, because Amy's hook was that you could win a case of gourmet chocolates from Lindt. Even without the hook, I think I would have clicked the URL, because if you love good food, acquiring a case of your treats is hog heaven, and Amy's clear definition of her site meant that I knew I wouldn't be wasting my time by visiting.

Another person whose business is defined in a few succinct words is Ali Kayn's Festivale Online Magazine. Ali is based in Melbourne, and the magazine covers events in the city. At the bottom of Ali's e-mail is a small signature file which reads: 'Festivale online magazine, Melbourne Australia'. Right away you know that the business is a magazine, it's probably entertainment-oriented (Festivale), you'll find information about Melbourne on the site, and probably some information about Australia as well.

To develop your business definition, think about:

- What best describes your business? Start by writing down some phrases which describe your business. Then write down the reason for its success, and the business's competitive strength.
- What's unique about your business?
- What benefits do your products or services give your customers?
- Brainstorm a name for your business's Web site which describes your business in a few words. You need a strong, clear image to which your Web site viewers can relate, and which they can locate when they use the Web search engines. Barry Michaels knows customers looking for boots will type 'boots' into search engines. Ann Zustak's What's in a Name is also a site which is easily retrieved by search engines.

2. What goals do you want to achieve?

It's definitely helpful to set goals for the online portion of your business. You may far exceed those goals, or you may not. But having those goals keeps you on track, moving in the direction in which you want your business to go. Start by writing down everything you want to achieve. Edie Davisson, of Edie's Herbals, was very clear about her goals. She had been growing organic herbs for sale in health-food stores in Victoria for ten years. Health problems meant that she had to give up her organic herb farm. However, she still wanted to keep her herb business, and she wanted to expand it globally via the Internet. She decided that rather than produce the herbs herself, she would use suppliers. She hoped that taking her business online would give her easier access to both customers and suppliers.

She says: 'One of my primary goals in taking the business online was saving money. Selling herbal products via mail order means investing around $8000—that's the cost of having a colour catalogue printed, and mailing the copies out to my customers.' Edie estimated that if she sold her herbals over the Internet, she could save on those printing and postage costs. Therefore, her original list of goals, which she hoped to achieve in her first year online, included:

- Save money.
- Keep serving the customers who have been with me for years.
- Develop additional suppliers—aim for five new suppliers.
- Develop new customers in the catering and hotel industries; aim for a 10 pre cent customer increase.

You can see that Edie's aims are focused. She knows how many new suppliers she wants, she also knows how many new customers she is aiming for.

After six months online, Edie has achieved and exceeded her goals, and also set new goals. She says that if she were taking her business online today, she would spend more time thinking about goals:

> I would have spent more time initially in thinking about and developing my goals—and I would have set them higher. Goals give you a direction, and energy. Now I realise I should have set a goal for a level of income for my first year, but I'm pleased with the goals I did set. I'm sure the online part of the business wouldn't have grown as quickly if I hadn't set those goals.

3. What business resources will you allocate to your online efforts?

Money and time are finite for all of us. Ideally, your online business plan will be part of the overall plan for your business. Creating a plan for taking your business online doesn't need to be complex. A simple one is much more useful. Stan Lourey's plan for his philatelist business was written on an index card:

When the lease ran out on my shop in a Sydney suburb, I didn't want to invest in another store. I'd already been selling stamps through various Internet newsgroups, and I've got friends with online businesses, so I knew what was involved in setting up online. I had an Internet connection, and my ISP now hosts my site.

Stan focused his business plan on money and time. He wanted to upgrade his computer, buy a faster modem, and hire someone to create his Web site. He put these costs onto the index card, and worked out how he would pay for them. He also budgeted to have someone create a database for him, and enter his collection of stamps into the database.

Although employing someone to create the Web site and the database cost money, it saved time. Stan says:

If I'd wanted to create the site myself, it still wouldn't be up. I went through all that. I've bought software programs and then never used them because I didn't have the time. Employing someone was more expensive, but I think I saved money in the long term. I was able to get my online store ready within a month of making the decision to do it.

When you take your business online, also think about the time your Web site will take to *maintain*. If you're working ten hours a day with offline activities, how will you budget the time to handle online business? Most of the people I spoke to spend at least an hour a day working with e-mail queries and orders. Some people, whose business was completely Web-based, spent considerably more.

When Marlene Shapiro took her secretarial business online, she found that maintaining her Web site, answering e-mail inquiries, and sending out invoices via e-mail didn't take more than ten to fifteen minutes per day. However, she saw the scope of online activities, and decided that she could make more money if she became a Web site designer. She now spends over six hours a day hooked up to the Internet, creating new Web sites and maintaining sites for her clients.

You won't know how long you'll spend in online activities until your Web site is up and running, but make an estimate of the time you think you'll need.

4. Develop your Web site

Your Web site can be as simple or as complex as you choose. A simple Web site may consist of a single page, stored on your ISP's server.

Although a single page can't contain a lot of information, it can include your business's address, your fax number, after-hours numbers, and trading hours. It can also include a small map, so that customers can find you more easily.

If you decide on a small site, you can create it in your word processor. However, larger sites are best created with specialist software if you plan on doing it yourself. If you don't have the time for this, then you can hire a Web site designer to do it for you.

5. Setting a launch date

Set a date to take your business online. You may not keep that date, but without it you'll find yourself engrossed in the everyday running of your business, and your online debut won't have the urgency required to keep your attention.

MAKE YOUR SITE INTERACTIVE

The Web is an interactive medium. Think of ways you can draw visitors into your site and encourage them to take some action which will further the aims that you have for the site. Here's a list of items you might include in your site:

- A form in which the user can register for something: an update to products, a newsletter, etc.
- A newsgroup-type discussion group—this could let visitors chat with your staff, or with other visitors to the site.
- Feedback forms which gather information. You can carry out surveys on the site, as well as testimonials which you can use in your marketing materials.
- Give-aways and freebies—always popular; a great way to get people to visit your site. This allows you to gather e-mail addresses, which you can use for product announcements later.
- A classified ads page. If you sell a product, people who are buying newer models might be wondering where they can sell the outdated one. Letting them post free classifieds on your site will attract visitors.

WILL YOU CREATE THE SITE YOURSELF, OR WILL YOU HIRE SOMEONE?

You've decided you want to develop a Web site for your business, but you're not sure whether you should do it yourself, or whether you should hire someone to do it for you. The benefit of doing it yourself is that you know your business. You know what you want to emphasise when it comes to creating an online image. No one you hire will have your expertise when it comes to your business.

Many of the people I spoke to created their own sites. Molly Gordon, fibre artist, and business and personal coach, is typical of those people who developed their own sites, and took a lot of pleasure in doing so. She took the time to learn about the technology involved, and this means that she isn't dependent on anyone else to maintain her electronic shopfront. She says that she values the ability to make changes to the site whenever she wants to, on her own schedule. 'I don't have to wait days or a couple of weeks for someone else to update the site.'

The Web site for Sareen Arabians is also the work of owner Talia Grey. 'I knew how I wanted the site to look. I felt that if I asked someone else to do it, I'd have to spend a lot of time explaining, plus making sure that the right description and pedigree went with the right photo, and so on.'

However, although you might want to do it yourself, this may not be practical. Creating a Web site takes time, and neither you nor your staff may have the time or energy to devote to creating a site. If this is the case, then you'll want to hire a Web site designer.

Your first question will be cost. How much? An average price for the creation of a site of around six Web pages, with electronic ordering, is $5000. You can pay less, but you can also pay much more. A good place to find local designers is on the newsgroups run by your ISP. Put up a message asking for freelance designers. Or, you can enter your location and 'Web site design' into one of the search engines— this should give you the Web addresses of dozens of designers.

Most designers have an online portfolio for you to look at. If you see sites that appeal, you can begin negotiations with the designer. Most designers are comfortable doing this via e-mail, and will be able to give you a quote on a preliminary design almost immediately. However, as well as looking at the portfolio, make sure that you visit the sites the designer has created. As you view the sites, look for more than visual appeal. Ask yourself whether a particular site sells. You should also check that the site is easy to navigate. If you wanted to buy a product shown on the site, would this be easy? In other words, is there an online order form and can you find it immediately?

When you've found a designer whose work you like, and whose prices fit into your budget, you should commission a preliminary proposal. This will give you a chance to see how good the designer is at following instructions. Does she grasp the essentials of your business? A reasonable price for a preliminary design would be around $1000. This includes the production of a sample site, with a couple of pages done in full, and an outline of what the other pages will cover.

You could also join a cybermall, which is a shopping mall on the Web. Cybermalls often have a theme, such as computer products, baby products or New Age products. If you're thinking about joining one, they will usually have their own in-house design team. Don't blindly sign up for this. There may be hidden charges, such as: additional fees for storage of the site, fees for registering your site with the major search engines, sending out media releases, charging for the number of hits you get to the site, and many more. You should also find out whether the design team updates the site regularly. If you want to include additional items in the database, will you be charged for this?

If the answers you get to any of your questions are less than satisfactory, look for someone else. Web design is a thriving industry. As with any new industry, however, there are people in it who care about what they do, and who do it well, as well as those who are only out to make a quick profit.

QUESTIONS TO ASK A DESIGNER CREATING YOUR WEB SITE

Before you approach a designer, think about what you want your Web site to do. You know your business best. The designer knows how to design. They don't know your business or your customers. Try to be clear in your own mind about what you want to achieve with the site.

Next, here are some questions to ask your designer:

• Have you designed for anyone else in my field?

- How do you work? Do you visit my business, or will I fax or e-mail the information to you?
- Do I get to choose the graphics?
- Are there additional charges for scanning photos?
- Will you give me a firm completion date?
- Do you have a standard agreement I could see?
- How much do you charge for site maintenance?
- Will you submit the site to search engines, and if so to how many?

DOING IT YOURSELF—CREATING YOUR FIRST WEB SITE

'I created my first site in three hours, on a rainy Sunday afternoon,' Peter McKenzie, a chess enthusiast says. 'It wasn't difficult. I used the Claris Home Page software, which cost around $50. I used one of the templates, which is a form, and just copied and pasted in my text. Then I added a couple of graphics I scanned into my computer from photos I'd taken, and the site was ready to go.'

Peter's initial aim was to share his love of chess with other Internet users. 'I created links to the best chess sites and game archives, and added a few thoughts of my own.' The response was 'phenomenal'. Peter laughs. 'I had to change ISPs. The site was getting around 2000 visitors a week, way more than my ISP could handle.'

Creating your own site is an option if:

- You don't have much cash, but you do have the time.
- You like to tinker.
- The site is reasonably simple in scope.

Finding a home for your Web site

These are your options when looking for a home for your site:

- On your own Web server.
- On your ISP's servers.
- At a Web site which offers free Web pages.
- At a cybermall.
- At a Web host's site.

We'll take these options in turn.

Hosting your site yourself on your own Web server

For most small businesses, hosting their Web site on their own server is both difficult and expensive. Someone in the company has to spend all their time managing the computer and the site; it's not a part-time job. Here's what you need: a computer to run the Web server software, the Web server software itself, which needs to be installed and configured by an expert, a high-speed Internet connection, a router, constant supervision of the setup, and much more. The starting price for all this? Somewhere around $10 000 and counting—which doesn't take into account salary or maintenance expenses, or the cost of the high-speed Internet access line. Some small business owners do maintain their own Web server, but the maintenance and the effort involved is a hobby; it's not making them any money. You'll have to decide whether this is an option for you.

Hosting your site on your ISP's servers

Many ISPs will let you create a small site, and post it on their servers, without charging you. If you've decided that you're happy with a small site, with only a couple of pages, then this could be the cheapest solution. There are several problems with this option, however, tempting as it may be to go for the freebie. The most significant problem is that smaller ISPs don't have secure servers, so you won't have the option to perform online transactions. Nor are small ISPs set up to handle thousands of visitors per day to any site they host; if your site is wildly successful, your ISP may ask that you take it elsewhere.

Web sites which offer free Web pages

Some ISPs don't have free Web pages available, but if you're on a small budget, you can get space at a free site. There are a mile of these on the Web. The best known are Geocities (www.geocities.com), Angelfire (www.angelfire.com) and Tripod (www.tripod.com). If these don't suit you, then just look for more via one of the search engines. Enter a query: 'free Web pages'. The free hosting services make money either by selling advertising space on the sites they host, or by providing site design services. If you run a SOHO operation, the larger free sites can be excellent options. They provide a sense of community, in that your site will be placed in an area with similar sites. This gives you the opportunity to network, and to find new customers and suppliers.

The free sites also save you time, because they use a template to help you set up your site. You can have your site set up and operational within half an hour. Just cut and paste data from your computer to their form, like Peter McKenzie did with his chess site, and you have an instant Web site. Using a template eliminates some of the hassles of Web site creation; you don't have to design the thing yourself, so you don't have to worry about fancy fonts and graphics, and you also don't have to worry about uploading the site to the server, because you simply enter the information into the appropriate boxes on the form, and then submit the form.

Cybermalls

Cybermalls aren't free services. They charge you to host your site at their mall. The benefits of cybermalls are:

- Someone from the mall will design your site, including e-commerce software, so you don't have the design/uploading/maintenance hassles.
- Promotion is included in your monthly fee.

As you might expect, there are problems with cybermalls as well:

- Their creation and design services can be very expensive, when compared to similar services on the Web. Some will charge you several hundred dollars for designing your (very small) site, when the going rate for similar services is under $200.
- It's often hard to find any evidence of active promotion of the mall itself, or of any of the sites outside the mall—many Web search engines don't index pages in cybermalls.

However, if you're a small business owner with a few hundred dollars to spend on getting a Web site, and don't want any of the concomitant hassles, then a cybermall can be a cost and time-effective solution. The most sensible way to decide on which mall might be right for your business is to contact your chosen mall's resident businesses via e-mail. Browse the mall, and copy any e-mail addresses you find into the Bcc: field in a new message. That way, you can contact ten people at the same time. Just type a brief message. You can ask what the residents think of the mall services, what their sales are like, whether they've had any problems—anything you can think of that would be good to know before you part with cash.

Web hosting services

Web hosting companies sell space on their computers to other companies that want to get onto the Web. In addition to providing space, they also provide services such as company e-mail, mail forwarding, online ordering and payment systems and complete web site design.

A Web hosting service is the ideal solution for many small companies. The benefits are:

- Your company can have its own domain name—more of which in a moment.
- It's as good as having your own Web server, but someone else has the hassles.
- Web hosting companies have lots of services for business sites, such as secure online transactions, and visit tracking.
- Web hosting services are usually inexpensive, when compared to options such as cybermalls, because of the number of sites they host.

Your own domain name (Internet address)

A domain name is basically your Internet address. Domain names are expressed as strings of numbers, and identify computers on the Internet. These numbers are associated with an 'alias', which is what users type into their browser. An Internet address which is readily identified with your business helps your current and potential clients find you easily and simply. Justin Magnan of inkjetrefills.com knows the value of the right domain name. His business is inkjetrefills.com, and his domain name, or Internet address, is www.inkjetrefills.com. If you have an ink jet printer, and wanted to buy refills on the Internet, you'd type 'ink jet refills' into one of the search engines, and Justin's business would pop up. Justin says: 'All of my business comes from the search engines. I get between 100 and 300 hits a day. I don't promote in any other way and, because my customers are actually searching for me, my inquiries to sales ratios are higher than those of most other Web sites.'

The beauty of your own domain name is that once it's yours, it's yours permanently—or at least as long as you pay the yearly registration fee. Catherine and Rolf C. Zimmerli of Switzerland started their Web business under someone else's domain. They found changing their URL to their own domain name was a real hassle. The Zimmerlis sell food supplements, such as vitamins, minerals and herbs, online. When they finally switched to their own domain, Rolf estimates that it cost the business some eighteen months to catch up to where it had been before—they were known under the old domain, and had to start building site traffic all over again with the new domain name. If they'd known about the benefits of their own domain name, they would have taken that option from the beginning of their online venture.

Therefore, even before you finish designing your Web site, you should think about the domain name you want, and take steps to register it. Don't hesitate too long. Domain names are reportedly being registered at the rate of around 17 000 a day. The system works very simply. When you type a domain name into your browser, the domain name is sent to a name server, which is a computer which stores a directory of domain names. The name server then finds the associated IP (Internet Protocol) number, and that number is used to send a message to the Web server.

Reasons for acquiring your own domain name

- You want your present customers to be able to find you by entering your company's name as the URL.
- Your company offers a unique product which they will expect to find via the search engines (such as ink jet refills in Justin's case).
- Your company owns registered trademarks or brand names, such as Kleenex, or Microsoft.

You want your company associated with a concept on the Web—such as ink jet refills, or whatever your primary business happens to be.

Acquiring the domain name of your choice will cost you around $100–$150, assuming that the domain name you've chosen is still available. The easiest way to check is to go to http://www.domainit.com, and enter the name you want into the Search dialogue box on the page. I tried it for Angela Booth, thinking it might be nifty to have my name as my domain name, and it was available.

Usually, when you make site-hosting arrangements with your ISP, or whoever you've chosen, they will offer to register a domain name for you. If you have a name which you *must* have (it's your company name), check with Domainit.com at the URL above to see whether it's still available. If it is, they'll reserve it for you, so that no other enterprising person snaps it up.

The information in this chapter should be enough to keep you thinking. In the next chapter, we'll get into the nuts and bolts of taking your business online.

chapter 3

Your business online

Let's look at what's involved in creating your site, including some Web authoring tools. We'll also think about the elements which make up an effective money-earning site, and the distracting elements you'll want to avoid. You need to hook your potential customers, so we'll look at ways to make your site enticing. Finally, we'll look at various kinds of businesses online and what elements they include in their sites.

CREATING YOUR SITE—AN OVERVIEW

Creating a 'Web site' sounds incredibly complex, but all you are doing, fundamentally, is creating an online presentation. 'You've created a presentation, haven't you?' is the first question Caterina Knopfler asks when her clients approach her about creating a Web site. Caterina runs a small advertising agency in Campbelltown, New South Wales. Her clients include real estate agencies and local car dealerships. She says:

> My clients don't have a budget for a Web site. Their promotions money is tied up in Yellow Pages advertising, and in advertising in local papers. When they ask me about creating their own Web site, I tell them not to be intimidated, just to look on it as creating a presentation—that's a concept that's easy to understand, and it gets across the fact that their site must have a purpose. And when I put it that way—just look on it

as a presentation—it becomes something that they're familiar with, something they can see themselves doing.

Caterina says she also describes the mechanics of creating the site. 'I tell them that their site exists as a directory on their own computer, as a set of hyperlinked HTML files. Then they copy those files to whoever is hosting the site for them. At that stage, their Web site has gone live. They're now on the Web.'

So in the first instance your site will exist on your own computer as a set of directories storing all the files, both HTML and graphics, you've created for the site. When you're happy with your efforts, you'll copy the site to whichever computer is hosting the site for you—usually a computer owned by your ISP, or by a Web hosting company. For example, on my hard disk on my work computer, I have a directory called *Angela's Creativity Web,* which contains all the files which make up my Web site of the same name. When I want to make changes to my site, I edit the files in *Angela's Creativity Web* and upload them to Zip, the ISP which hosts my site. Zip has an *Angela* directory, which contains all the files which make up my Web site. Zip's version is a mirror—a copy—of the files on my own computer. Whenever I upload my *Angela's Creativity Web* directory to Zip, the current files replace the old files.

Now comes the exciting part: the actual creation of the pages which will make up your site. Creating the site is a simple process; here it is in outline:

1. Create the pages which make up the site. You can do this in your word processor, or in various web authoring packages.
2. Collect the files you've created, including the graphics, onto a single directory on your hard disk. If you use a Web authoring package, the program will do this for you.
3. Check the files for spelling mistakes, and ensure that they have links to each other. Your home page should have links to the other main pages of the site. If you use a comprehensive Web authoring package, like Microsoft FrontPage, you will be able to check the links while the site is still on your computer. FrontPage includes a cut-down version of Web server software, which means that you can browse the pages of the site exactly as if they were already on the Internet.
4. When you're sure that everything works as it should, it's time to

upload everything to your Web hosting company, or whoever is hosting the site. You may need to do this manually, with an FTP (File Transfer Protocol) package. If you use a program like Front-Page, the program uploads the files for you automatically.

5. When the site has been saved to its new home, you can connect to the Internet and check your site. This is the time to find out how quickly the site loads, and whether there are any final modifications you want to make. Ask colleagues and customers to check the site at this stage too. You want as many people as possible to log on, using various different computers and browsers, so you can see how the site performs for them.

The pages which make up the site

Whatever kind of site you intend creating, here are the basic elements which make up the majority of Web sites:

1. A home page: that is, a main entry page. Every Web site has a 'home' or 'index' page, something like the table of contents in a book. The home page tells the visitor what the site's purpose is, what they will find on the site, and how to locate the information. Your home page should be free of clutter, but it should also provide useful information. Don't devote the page to a huge graphic; if you do, many of your visitors will leave before the graphic has a chance to download.
2. A sales area: the catalogue of goods or services which your business offers.
3. An order form: make sure that your catalogue has a way for your customers to place their orders, and make this order form *highly visible*.
4. A customer-support area: this is where people can find more detailed information about your products. You could also put troubleshooting information here, and information on where to locate accessories for your products. For example, if you sell sewing machines, you could put solutions for common problems here, the addresses of service centres, and addresses of people selling sewing cabinets.
5. A feedback page: this is vital. The Internet offers an easy way for you to find out more about your customers. Use a form here to

take surveys, source new product ideas, find out why some of your products are selling better than others, and so on.

This is the time to go and look at your competitors' sites on the Web. How have they presented their information? Are their sites done well, or not? How can you make your site better? Since you are in the process of creating your own site, you will find that you look at others' sites in a new way. You may even find that you appreciate others' sites more.

Building your first Web site: the mechanics

Creating a Web site used to be complex. It meant learning HTML, which although not difficult, took time. To serve the requirements of those people who just wanted to get their site on the Web, and were not interested in learning the ins and outs of HTML, a whole new group of software tools emerged: HTML editors. These tools are now as simple as word processors; no programming experience is necessary.

The two leading programs at the moment are Claris Home Page, and Microsoft FrontPage. The Claris product is around $100, the Microsoft around $200. (If you're penny-pinching, you can browse shareware sites on the Web, and download a free Web authoring tool called Arachnophobia.)

If you just want to create a simple 'billboard' site, with only a couple of pages of text and some graphics, the Claris product is ample for your needs. It comes with a range of templates—forms which you simply fill with your own text, and select fonts, colours and textures to give a professional look to the site. On the other hand, if you envision that you'll want the works—a big site with many pages and lots of bells and whistles, such as links to your product database and online ordering, FrontPage is your program. FrontPage comes with a lot more templates than Home Page, and you can customise these templates to suit your business.

Your Claris Home Page Web site should take you around half an hour to set up. If you're using Microsoft FrontPage, count on an afternoon to create the basics of your site. You'll want another day or so to experiment if you're adding online ordering facilities to your site.

Collect the files you've created

Keep a list of the files you create for the site somewhere, or get into the habit of saving all new files for the site in the same place: a single directory. You can then upload the entire directory at once. This isn't always possible. For example, if you're a real estate agent, your scanning software may have a directory where it saves the photos you scan into your computer. If this is the case, make a list of the files you need, and collect copies of them into the same directory. If you've used a Web authoring product, like Home Page or FrontPage, this won't be a problem. Both programs will automatically create directories to store your files.

Check the files for spelling mistakes and other nasties

Spelling mistakes on a Web site are a common problem. Check the pages you're created carefully. Spell checkers are a start, but you should also proofread the pages yourself.

You will also want to check that the photos you want to put up look good in several different kinds of browsers. All browsers handle colour somewhat differently, and a page which looks great in Internet Explorer may look horrible in Netscape. If you're a real estate agent, for example, you don't want to put up photos which are so dark that no one knows what they are, so check that both Netscape and Internet Explorer display your photos well.

Hints to remember for creating an effective, selling Web site

- Web surfers don't read: they scan. Eliminate extra words and 'fluff'. Make your Web copy sharp and to the point—think 'nuggets' of information, rather than slabs of text.
- No large graphics—please.
- Have your contact details on every page.
- Keep your pages small. Your visitors will press the Page Down button on their computer keyboard no more than twice; if they don't find what they want by then, they're out of there.
- Site graphics—do you need them at all? Graphics are a contentious issue on the Web. The easiest way to decide whether your site needs graphics is to ask yourself whether the graphic you want to add does anything useful. For example, if you're selling a house, potential buyers need to see the place, so the photo of the house serves a useful purpose. Ditto for any other physical object you want to sell: your buyers want to see what they get. If your graphics are there simply to set a mood, or because you like them, drop them.

Upload your site

Now's the big moment, uploading all the files which make up your site to the computer which will present the site to the world. This is a simple copying job. If you've used FrontPage to create the site, the program will do the job of uploading (called 'publishing' by FrontPage) when you tell it to do so. If you've used another program to create your pages, you'll have to use an FTP (File Transfer Protocol) program to move the files. Shareware sites on the Web, such as ZDNet (www.hotfiles.com), provide several programs, some of them free for the downloading.

Test your site

As soon as you've uploaded the files, try out your site. Access it via your browser, just as any visitor would do. Do all the links work? Do your forms work? You may see problems, but don't be discouraged—this is only to be expected. And this is your chance to fix those problems before you promote the site and start attracting visitors in bulk. For example, you may find that the photos you've taken are too dark, or the site is too large horizontally, so that viewers need to scroll to the right. Take a few days to work out the kinks in the site. You should also ask your clients to take a look at the site, and tell you about any problems which they have with it.

CREATING AN EFFECTIVE WEB SITE

Creating a Web site is easy, but creating a Web site which is effective takes some thought and experimentation. Online publication is not print, nor is it television or radio. Online publication is a new medium, with its own requirements. Online publication means working with hypertext—with linked documents. It's an active medium: the user selects their own information, as much or as little as they want. They are free to click and go wherever they want to. They have options which are simply not available with paper or with TV.

Knowing that your viewer always has the option to escape, you have some decisions to make:

1. How should you present your information? Ideally, you should provide it in related fragments, not in large slabs. You'll notice from your own viewing of sites that you tend to skim, rather than

read the information carefully. Make it easy for your visitors to do this. However, you should also offer more detailed information for those people who want it.

2. How many routes through that information should you provide? Too many links on a page are distracting. However, if you provide too few, visitors may miss important areas of your site.

3. How much information should you provide? You need to think carefully about what information is most important.

4. Should you provide links to other sites from your site? Links are popular, yet if you make the links too noticeable, and if they seem more interesting than your site, you're making escape easy.

Of course, there is no 'right' answer to any of these questions. Most importantly, your Web site must be useful; you won't attract visitors by presenting an online brochure. The more useful your site is to people, the more visitors you will get, and therefore the more products you will sell. Always ask yourself two questions about anything you place on your site: Is this useful for my visitors? Is this providing a benefit for my business?

For superb examples of effective Web sites, try these sites, which review the best of the Web:

• Best of the Web: http://www.botw.org
• Web 500: http//www.web500.com/categories/Links/links.html

How should you present your information?

You should present your information in as interesting a way as possible; however, you don't need to dazzle your visitors with streaming video and audio, and animated graphics. In fact, if you go overboard with the special effects, rather than dazzling your visitors you're likely to annoy them.

Bernice Werber consults on Web site design for small businesses. She advises:

Think of your customers. What do they expect to find when they come to your site? If you're a company which sells camping equipment, for example, they expect to find tents and bedrolls, so concentrate on showing your wares. Don't go for huge graphics of outdoor scenes—the Web is not a magazine. If people want to see superb graphics of mountains and jungles, let them go to the Sierra Club site or the National

Geographic site. If you're selling camping equipment, then show that equipment. Everything you put on your site should benefit your visitor in some way.

Multimedia and plug-ins—only if you need them

Multimedia are sounds, videos, radio; plug-ins are various attachments you can install into your browser so that you can see, hear, and experience special effects. While these can be useful, you should think carefully about whether they're necessary, and you should always provide alternatives to using them.

It's annoying for your customers to come to your site, and to read that they need ShockWave or some other browser plug-in before they can watch a presentation. You can offer the ShockWave presentation, but you should also offer an alternative—perhaps you could send the presentation on CD-ROM to those people who don't have time to watch it on the Web.

Several Australian real estate sites use multimedia brilliantly. A great example is the McGrath & Partners site at http://www.mcgrath.com.au/index1.html. This site features virtual tours of properties. David Logan, Web developer of John Fairfax Holdings, explained how the virtual tours are created: 'We use a combination of Quicktime VR encoded images, flat photographs, and pre-recorded streaming Real Video.' Virtual Tours are a case of multimedia adding value to a site: the viewers save time. They have a chance to take a tour of a property within a few minutes, saving hours of time travelling to the actual site, taking the real tour, and then learning that the property wasn't for them. If you can use multimedia as effectively as the McGrath & Partners site, go for it.

Real world metaphors—avoid them

You've seen these sites, which are supposed to portray the everyday world. Cybermalls are often set up like this. They present a graphic of a town or a city, and the buildings have the names of the cyberstores which make up the site. The problem with such sites is that the graphics take a lot of time to load, and don't add any information that the visitor needs. Simply the names of the businesses, with their business logo, would appear in a fraction of the time, and would achieve the same objective.

How many routes through your site's information should you provide?

Do you want your visitors to move through your site quickly, or do you want them to linger? If you have a great many products to sell, if your site is an online bookstore for example, or a car dealership, you want people to spend time at your site so that you can sell them your products. However, if you're providing customer support for your products, you don't want to keep people—you want them to find the information they need quickly.

You provide the routes through your site via hypertext links. If your aim is to sell products, you want visitors to gain as much exposure to the product as possible. Think about how your site is structured, or how it will be structured if you haven't yet created it. Make the structure logical, so that your visitors can find the information they came for; however, don't make it too easy for them to find the data they want—you don't want them to miss additional information you want to show them.

How much information should you provide?

If you're selling something on your site, you need enough information for buyers to come to a decision. If you're using the site to promote your offline business, you need to convince your visitors to get out of their homes and offices and climb into their cars so they can make the trip.

Should you provide links to other sites from your site?

Good links are useful. They can lend credibility to your site, and to your business, if your business is new. However, don't make the links too accessible. Don't put them on the home page. Bury the links a couple of levels deep in the site, unless you have a good reason to do otherwise.

HOOKING YOUR CUSTOMERS

When people locate your site using InfoSeek or Yahoo, yours may be the only site they come up with. Perhaps you're the only person in the world who sells reproduction Victorian mourning brooches, for example. However, it's more likely that your site will be in a list of dozens, if not hundreds of similar sites. So what will make your site stand out enough to draw the crowd?

One way to draw people to your site is to buy advertising space on the major search engines, so that when people type in a query, your banner ad is displayed above the search results. An easier, less expensive way is to develop a Unique Selling Point. What have you got that no one else has, or what do you do that no one else does?

Think about your hook, or USP, by asking yourself these questions:

- What makes people choose my site from a long list?
- If my site were to be reviewed in a magazine, what would the reviewer say about it?

If you don't have a hook, you need to brainstorm until you do have one. Here's a sampling of generic hooks:

- You're the leader in your field. *We're the: largest/best/most awarded/have been in business longest/have the biggest range etc.*
- You offer what the others don't. *We provide: same-day service/home delivery/drive-through service/3-year guarantee etc.*
- You offer added benefits. *We provide free installation etc.*

Respond quickly

The Web gives you a unique opportunity to see your customers as individuals—you can respond to their particular needs, and this increases the opportunity you have to make a sale. Make it easy for your site's visitors to tell you what they want. Put your e-mail link in a prominent place on *every* page of the site, so that they can e-mail you. When you receive an e-mail message, it's vital that you send a response as soon as you can, at least within 24 hours. If you don't have the information, product or service the customer wants, tell the customer when it will be available. If you don't respond quickly to messages sent to you, you will be perceived as slow. Ergo, your product or service will be perceived in the same way. If a customer visiting your site places an order via the site for 50 widgets, and you're all out of widgets, respond immediately to explain.

You also need to be fast in delivering your customer's goods once they've ordered them. Your offline customers may be willing to wait three weeks or longer for you to deliver. Your Web customers won't be. They expect you to be fast: aim to deliver by overnight courier if possible, or at the most within five working days. In some cases, you may not know whether the item the customer wants is available or not, or you may have to order it in. Powells Bookstore, at URL: http://www.powells.com, is an online bookseller with a range of both new and used books. They have several physical stores in addition to their Internet services, and although books may be in the Web database, they may be out of stock when the Internet customer places the order. Powells make this clear on their page—they explain that a response may take a few days, until they physically locate the books the customer wants to order. When I order from Powells, I know that I will have to wait to learn whether the books are still available, and that's fine, because I know that up-front.

Many businesses fail to capitalise on their Web sites. You can visit a site three times, over a period of many months, and not one change has been made to the site. Nor is there any overt sign that they want visitors to respond—if there is an e-mail link, there's only one, and that's to the Webmaster (the site creator/manager). Customers want to interact with the sales or service department, not with the Webmaster.

Build as much interactivity into your site as you can. Look at Harris Technology (URL: http://www.ht.com.au) for a good example of how this can be done.

And be responsive.

WHAT BENEFITS DOES YOUR SITE GIVE ITS VISITORS?

It's no longer enough simply to have a Web page. The page has to be useful—it has to show your customers immediately what benefits they will gain from doing business with you. Often Web page designers become so caught up in the technology, that a Web site seems to be more about animations and glitzy effects than about anything else. To make the sale, make the benefits obvious.

Greg Bacia feels that the simplest sites can often be the most effective, as long as they focus on the benefits to the customer:

Keep it simple. The customer's needs are paramount—you don't have to do more than focus on those needs. However, visitors to the site have to see the benefits *immediately*: the benefits shouldn't be buried five pages deep into the site. Put your good stuff up-front. We put auction information on the first page, and it's updated daily.

49

If, like Greg, you're a real estate agent, you want your visitors to be able to find the home of their dreams. You'll need to get your database up on your site so that visitors can see your listings. Greg said:

In a way, I was lucky. I knew what my intentions were. I just wanted to help my wife and put her listings online. That meant that the database was primary. It was my focus, and we were the first in our area to put listings online. Whenever I'm tempted to tinker with the site and put a large graphic on the first page, I ask myself whether it will benefit the customers. If it doesn't, then I don't do it.

No matter what your business, the major benefit to the customer of doing business with you online will be convenience. It's easier to browse an online database of property listings, for example, than it is to drive to the estate agent's office and go through the listings there.

Greg emphasises that you have to keep thinking like the customer if you are to create an effective site. If he were creating a new real estate site, Greg says that he would aim to make it as convenient as possible for the site's visitors to find the kind of home they want. This means that the database also needs to be easy to query.

Greg also recommends that you make it easy for clients to inspect the properties they're interested in:

Make it as easy as possible for them. My wife and I pick up our clients at their office or home, and take them out for property inspections at times that suit them—six in the morning, or seven in the evening, if those are the times which are most convenient for the customer. Motivating people who see a property online to take action is simple if you make it easy and convenient for them to do it.

As a first step to knowing what benefits you want to give your customers in your own site, visit lots of other sites developed by businesses which are similar to your own. What benefits does the site give the customer? Does the site make these benefits obvious? Can you see what the benefit is to the customer on the first page of the site? Think about what questions you have that the site doesn't answer—does the site make it easy (e-mail link, phone or fax number) to get answers to those questions?

If you sell anything tangible, then pictures are a vital part of your site. These are a benefit to the customer. For example, if you sell antique pens, as Charles Montfort of The Gilded Pen does, you'll want to get pictures of your collection of items onto the site. The benefit for the customer is convenience again. The customer can see exactly what you're selling. Charles says that reading a description of a 1910 pen won't do as much for your potential clients as actually seeing the item will. 'If I put up a picture of an item, I know that it will sell within the next couple of weeks. No picture, and the sale takes longer.' He admits that he tries to keep a balance between lots of graphics and a site which is fast-loading. 'If you have too many graphics on a page, that page will take longer to load. People with slower computers won't hang around. I put up as many graphics as possible, while I make sure that the pages load fast.'

However, as well as pictures, you should also include text. A photo on a PC monitor isn't as clear as it would be in a glossy magazine, and it can't be compared to seeing and touching the item. Your text should entice the customer: give them details about the item, focusing on the benefits. To move them from pausing to read to pausing to buy, you need to motivate them by being absolutely clear about the benefits. This is far from easy to do, and it may mean getting professional help. You may want to consider hiring a professional photographer and copywriter to produce the images and copy for your site.

Greg Bacia does his own photography and hires a copywriter:

> I think smooth descriptions of the houses make the site more professional. People buying a house are buying a dream. On the Web site, we try to give them an honest description of the homes, but we also try to convey that each house has a special quality. I can't write like that.

Beware of telling your clients too much

One way of showing the benefits of your product or service is to give your online visitors information. But you need to be wary of telling your prospective clients too much, especially if you're in a service business. If you give them all the information they need, they may decide to do the job themselves.

Debbie Saylor of Saylor Editorial Services warns that some Web sites may be doing themselves out of business:

> You need to put information up on your site, so that visitors will linger, and also because that's the Internet culture. People expect free information.

However, we learned the hard way that you can tell people too much. When we first developed the site, we put templates online for press releases, business letters, product announcements, and so on. They were to show what we could do.

Debbie found that people were using the free information on the site, but didn't use the business services:

We overcame that, by making the templates shareware. After they've tried the templates, if they want to keep them, we ask them to pay us $20. We know that many people never bother to register, but many do. And the fact that they've paid us for something which they use seems to have a good psychological effect. At least half our new clients say that they came to us to write their company report, or product announcement or whatever, because they use our shareware templates.

Debbie feels that the templates are a benefit to the customer which are drawing people to the site. Using the templates keeps the company's name in the customers' minds, and they hire Saylor Editorial Services when they need editorial help.

Daimon Reilly is a business consultant, and he also warns against putting too much information onto your site and providing too much information for free:

We used to give free initial consultations. We figured this was a real and tangible benefit to the customer. It also built up our credibility, so that people would know who we were, that we could help them, and how we could do that. However, the initial consult usually included a plan of action for the business. Many people took the free consult, and the plan we developed for them, and never came back to us. In fact, several times I learned that they had gone to another business consultant, rather than coming back to us. Since we always put in around an hour of research, and then wrote the plan for their business—and there's the time spent in phone calls, e-mail, and so on—we gave a lot away.

Now Daimon says that they provide references from current and former satisfied clients rather than giving free consultations. 'The benefits to our clients are still the primary focus of the site. We show visitors what we can do for them by showing what we've done for others.'

BUSINESSES CURRENTLY ONLINE

When you plan your site, it isn't necessary to follow what everyone else in your particular business is doing: look at sites from many different kinds of businesses to get ideas. Your aim isn't to be different from others in your industry for the sake of being different; your aim is to create an effective site that your customers remember and return to.

Remember your customers. That's vital. Your customers are the people who will tell you what they'd like to see on your site. Ask them. The easiest way to do this is to make up a questionnaire. You can send the questionnaire out to all your customers, or you can leave it near the cash register to give to customers as they leave. Again and again, the people who have successfully taken their business online told me that they gave their customers what they asked for, and it worked for them. Look at the first few months of developing your Web site as a learning experience: *ask your customers what they want to see on your site!* When your site is operational, keep asking your customers whether the site works for them, and what else they would like to see on your site.

Your restaurant online

A restaurant draws customers from the local area. If your restaurant is in Sydney, you'll draw customers from Sydney. Therefore, your Web site can be minimalist: the restaurant's name, address, phone number, and opening times. If you want to include more, consider also including a map of your location, so that diners can find you easily. This is especially important if you're off the beaten track. Other items you can add include the menu, with graphics of various dishes, newspaper reviews if you have them—anything that will draw diners to you. For example, the Glenella restaurant in the Blue Mountains of New South Wales has an excellent site. It shows the menu, and photos of the restaurant and the countryside, and gives some of the restaurant's history as well. An excellent map to the location is provided—it's easy for patrons to print the map, so they know they won't get lost.

Your menu is important. If I'm in the mood to eat out, I'll study the menus of various restaurant sites, and from asking around I know that others do this as well. Nothing is more important than your menu—it's why your customers go to your restaurant to eat. You'll want to give your menu pride of place on your site, as Beppi's restaurant in Sydney does. You don't need to include graphics of every item on the menu. However, you should include your specialty, as well as some mouth-watering descriptions. Edna's Table in Sydney specialises in Australian bush tucker—wild foods—and you quickly realise this from the site, which has some great descriptions of the food, as well as good graphics.

If the restaurant has received a favourable review in a magazine or a newspaper, you'll definitely want to include that on the site. However do make sure that you get permission first, because the review will be copyrighted. If you don't have any reviews, then consider contacting one of the online directories, such as Citysearch (URL: http://sydney.citysearch.com.au), to do a review.

For the convenience of visitors to the site, you might consider putting an online reservation form on your site. This can be as simple as an e-mail link, which does mean that you will need to check your e-mail several times a day.

If you have special events at the restaurant, such as live music, fashion shows or wine tastings, you can announce these on the site. You could also make it easy for your customers to hear about upcoming events by getting them to sign up for e-mail announcements.

Think about what you want your customers to know. Is your restaurant smoke-free? Do you offer low-fat options for diners on a diet? Do you serve vegetarian dishes? Perhaps you have some recipes which customers ask for; if so, place them on the site.

Your mail-order business online

The Internet is ideal for mail-order businesses. You cut down on printing costs for your brochures and catalogues, and you also cut down on expensive advertising costs. However, in spite of the benefits, there is one major stumbling block. Although people like to look at online offers, getting them to take the plunge and place an order is a challenge. You need to convince your visitors that you run a reputable business, and most of all that they will benefit from ordering online.

The first step in gaining credibility is to provide enough information for your customers to contact you *offline*. You should include your business address, and a phone number. This can be difficult if you run your business from home, or if you don't have the staff to answer the phone. Peter Nelson sells mobile phones and accessories online. He says:

> We advertise only in the Yellow Pages and on our Web site. This year, half our business has come from our Web site. However, although we have online ordering, only 10 per cent of our customers place their order online. Most seem more comfortable making a phone call and talking to a salesman, and then placing the order over the phone.

Peter believes that customers' willingness to place an order online is related to the cost of the item. 'People will order a book, a CD or even flowers online without giving it much thought. But when it comes to ordering high-ticket items, they like to know who they're dealing with.'

Additional credibility is given when you include some information about yourself (with a photo), and some information about your business. How long have you been in operation? What is your business's mission? If you feel that this is overkill—you can point to dozens of businesses online that don't do this—ask your customers. Ask them what would persuade them to do business with someone on the Internet. When you've convinced your online visitors that they're dealing with a real business, you can concentrate on displaying your products. You'll need to display photos of your products. If you have a large range, then you can present the range as an online catalogue, with some graphics as well as descriptions of the products. Since the problem with a graphics-intensive site is that the graphics take time to download, you might want to provide just the descriptions and the prices of the products first. Add a hyperlink (clickable icon) for each product. Then your visitors can choose what they want to look at in detail.

With mail order, spend some time thinking about why your customers shop in this way. Jean Kavelle sells mail-order cosmetics from her Southern Beauty site, and says that from her experience, online mail-order operators don't take their customers into consideration as much as they should:

> Price and convenience are the key words to keep in mind. The customer needs to be convinced of the quality of the product, and that it's available at a good price. If you have a product which is unique, that helps as well. People order online because it saves them a trip to the shops.

Your service business online

What if you own a business that involves working in your customers' homes? In this case, you'll want to provide all the usual information: your location, hours you work, and so on. If you offer a round-the-clock, seven-days-a-week service, you should of course display this prominently.

In this kind of business, trust is vital. You need to assure your customers that you know all you need to know about building, landscaping, plumbing, electricity, or whatever your service happens to be. You can do this by providing your licence number, if a licence is required. You can also display how many years you've been in business. Or, if you're just starting out, think about the assets you have. Why should your customers call you? Do you have the latest equipment? Do you sell washing machines as well as repair them?

Now that your customers know who you are, tell them something about your work. If you're a landscape gardener, provide some photos and full descriptions of gardens you've landscaped, and some customer referrals. If you sell products as well as providing a service, give descriptions, images, prices, and an order form.

You can make your site more useful to your customers if you provide additional information and links. But be careful that this material isn't just a jumble. Your information should be something that the customer needs to know, and your links should relate to your business. For example, A Cleaner Carpet Web site provides links to Du Pont carpets, as well as links to other businesses in a variety of areas, all connected in some way to carpets.

Your real estate business online

Australian real estate sites on the Web vary in size. You'll find small sites developed by agents themselves, such as the Lin Andrews Real Estate site. You'll also find large database sites, such as REALNET and RealWeb, featuring properties listed by hundreds of agents. However, buying a house isn't as simple as buying a bunch of flowers or a book, and you wouldn't conduct the entire process online—although Kevin Clay of REALNET believes that you will be able do that in a couple of years.

REALNET is a service of the Real Estate Agents' Cooperative. Not all member agents in New South Wales, Queensland, Western

Australia and New Zealand have all their properties online as yet, but Kevin Clay, the chairman of the board of REALNET, hopes that they soon will. All members of the EAC can put their properties online. He says that the main benefits for the buyers are: 'They don't need to walk out of their front door. They can find exactly the property they want, and they can compare properties, all without leaving home.' Kevin Clay says that the response of Internet users to the REALNET site has been 'phenomenal':

> It's much greater than we expected. When we first put up the site, we treated it as an exercise, and didn't expect much of a response since we didn't advertise the site, either online or offline. However, when we saw that the average time that surfers were spending at the site was 13–14 minutes, we knew that these were people who were very interested— they weren't casual surfers.

The Web works as a selling medium for real estate. REALNET ran a test. They put a North Sydney property online which was owned by a staff member. The property was listed nowhere else. Kevin Clay says: 'There were so many inquiries, including from overseas, that we ended up selling the property at auction. It achieved a much higher price than we expected. The only advertising for the auction was a listing online, and we ran a small ad in the local paper.'

Mark Woschnak of RealWeb believes that some 15 per cent of Australian real estate agents are now online:

> The problem is that many agents are not aware of what the technology can do for them. No agent who's seen RealWeb has failed to be excited by the potential. RealWeb saves agents time and money, in that it includes listing management functions, listing tools and a search engine, as well as marketing tools.

RealWeb was launched in late 1997, and is the flagship service of InfoWave, a wireless and intranet communications company. Mark Woschnak says of RealWeb: 'Some 200 agents have committed to listing with us so far. We offer them complete control over their listings. They have their own ID and password, and not only can they update their listings whenever they like, they can also list as many properties as they like.'

Mark also believes that agents find RealWeb cost-effective: agents pay a flat monthly fee of $200 to list an unlimited number of

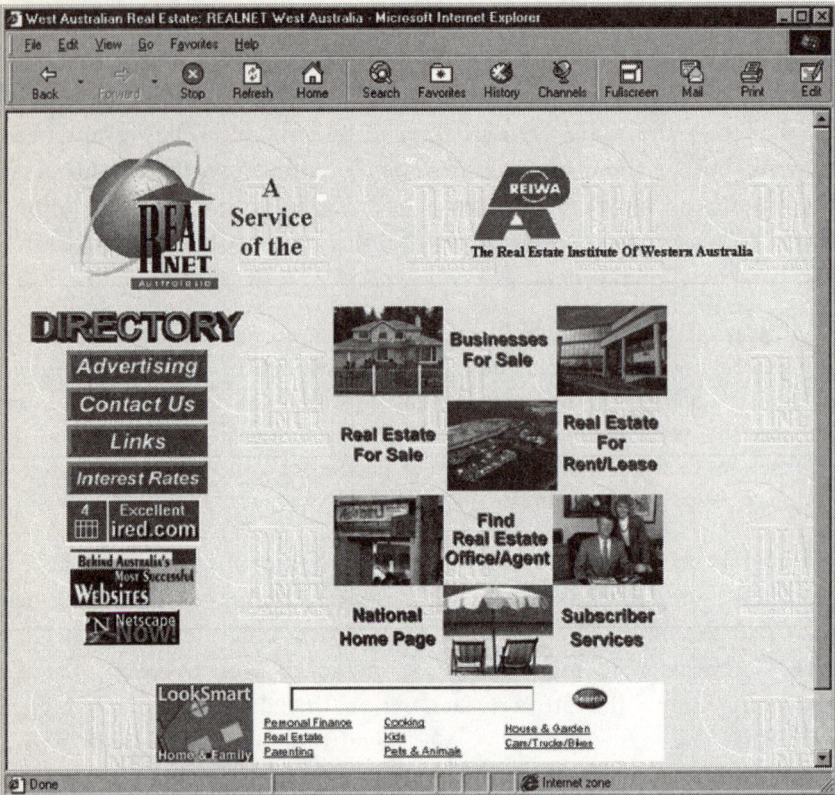

REALNET: a real estate agents' cooperative. Real estate agents are prominent among the many small businesses in Australia that have set up Web sites.

properties. 'We have exciting developments planned. We'll have video streaming, with voice-over, digital mapping, and 3D virtual reality.'

Developing their own Web site, rather than joining a group site, gives agents the chance to develop a brand image for their site. However, Lin Andrews believes that while some agents are initially enthusiastic about their Web site, they fail to realise that developing and launching a Web site is only the first step. 'Updating is costly, and many agents who are new to the online environment fail to realise that you need to be meticulous in updating the site. If you leave properties online which have sold, you're quickly found out and you lose credibility.' However, he believes that the return on investment makes the cost of maintaining a site worthwhile:

The two beachside properties that I sold to clients who found them online had been on our books for twelve months. They're just two sales that I know of personally which would not have sold unless they were online. Our staff have many more examples of properties that sold because they were online.

Whatever your business, visit other sites in your profession or industry to see how they present their business online. Then plan your site, always taking your customer's needs, and the benefits to them, into account as you plan.

chapter 4

Your business as home page—your shopfront to the world

This chapter contains information to help you to create a site to which your visitors will return with pleasure. It assumes that you've already created your site. In the last chapter, we covered the basics of creating a Web site, and this is what you should do, without delay. A Web site which works for your business is created piece by piece; you learn what works by doing it.

Creating an effective site is an ongoing challenge. A Web site is never completed. You will be changing the site on a weekly, or at least a monthly basis. Indeed, many business owners work on their site every day, adding new information and removing anything which has become outdated. One of the biggest benefits of a Web site is its immediacy: your clients will tell you what they want to know, and you can insert the information right away. For example, if you own a real estate agency, your clients might tell you that they would like to see floor plans of the homes. You can scan the plans, and add them to the site.

YOUR SITE'S USEABILITY

What makes a site useable? You no doubt have some ideas on this already, based on sites you've seen. Let's finetune your site, and make it more useable for your visitors. Useability starts with thinking about the concept behind your site, and emphasising it.

The concept

Think concept. What's the key idea behind your site? You should be able to express the concept in a single sentence. For example:

* If you own a nursery, what's unique about your nursery? Perhaps you specialise in roses—are you an authority on roses?
* If you own a hardware store, what's unique about your store? What benefits does your store offer over other hardware stores? Perhaps you stock a wide range of house paints, and offer a colour-matching service?
* Perhaps your site is a public service facility. For example, a site which is devoted to information for people who want to lose weight is a public service site. What's unique about your site—what makes your site different from other sites offering weight-loss advice? Do you have a kilojoule counter online? A meal planner?

Note on public service sites: More and more of these information-only, public service sites are being created by canny business people. The revenue stream in these public service sites is in advertising. A site such as the weight-loss example would attract advertisers from the weight-loss and health industries. Some of these sites are hugely popular; if you offer something which is related to the site's subject matter, consider advertising on such a site.

It's vital that you're clear about the concept behind your site. Write your concept out, in no more than 25 words. Look on it as your site mission statement. Give a copy to your designer, and to anyone advertising on, or creating content for, your site.

Your concept is important because:

* It differentiates your site from a mass of similar sites.
* It forces you to focus on your visitors.
* It's easier to promote your site if you can describe the concept behind it in a few words.

The most important things to remember about Web site layout

After your concept, the layout is the most important aspect of your site. But shouldn't you worry about the layout before you create your site? No—the most important thing is to get your site online. Layout looms large in many people's thinking, usually to the detriment of content. Some people worry so much about how their site looks that they forget that it's supposed to be doing a job. You can work on your layout when you have feedback from the people who are visiting your site.

In thinking about the layout, think about your target audience. What is the demographic? You want the site to be useful for many people, but you must know the demographic you want to attract so that you can keep them in mind. Formally write out a description of your target audience. When you first put your site up, ask for comments from your audience. Think of this as your own online focus group. Create a questionnaire for them to fill in, so that you can see what changes you need to make. Ask: do you find the site easy to navigate? Did you find the order form quickly? What's unclear about the site?

As you think about layout, a pen and paper is your most useful planning tool. Make rough sketches of the layout of the home page, as well as other pages. This lets you see how the viewers will move around the site. It also makes sure that you don't forget vital items, such as an e-mail link, and the prices of the products and services you're offering. Don't laugh; as you click your way around the Web, you'll find many sites which don't have prices or even contact information. If you've missed adding some of this info, add it now. When you make the sketches, use coloured pencils or pens, and shade in the background. *Note:* keep your site's background pale, and use black for all text. Bright backgrounds and pale text are difficult to read.

Don't annoy your visitors

Web page designers (especially graphics artists) can become very caught up in the design. This is understandable. However, it can also lead to loss of business if potential customers hate the site so much they won't spend any time there. Think this is a bit strong? Trust me, it isn't. Here's what will annoy visitors:

- **Background images.** The reason Web designers insert background images onto pages is to improve the look of the site. Sometimes they get lucky, and the background image *isn't* distracting and annoying. However, that's not usually the case. When your designer offers you a background image, or inserts an image without consulting you, just say *no*. If you're doing the designing, and you want to include an image, don't. People access the Web using computers of varying vintages and capabilities. Your site with its complex background images may look fantastic on your machine, and on your designer's machine, but it's unlikely that anyone using a slow 486 would have the patience to wait around for a large background image to load, let alone the rest of the content—and the background image always loads first.

- **Fonts.** Stick with Times New Roman and its clones for body text, and Helvetica and clones for headings. Avoid script fonts, and other way-out fonts. Even if selling fonts is your business, you should stick with the most readable fonts for your site's content, and offer samples of the exotics as image files. This is because Web browsers don't download fonts from the Web, they use the fonts which are on the computer on which they're running.

- **Frames.** Frames are panels that open in your browser's window at some Web sites. The panel on the left (or on the top or the bottom) usually contains a clickable page of contents for the site. Although frames are ubiquitous, and useful, you shouldn't use them indiscriminately. Again, remember that people will be loading your site onto their own equipment. A framed site usually loads a number of pages into a single browser window. Theoretically, this makes it easier for the viewer to navigate the site. However, a group of pages takes longer to load than one page, and your viewers may decide not to bother waiting.

- **Cookies.** Not the biscuit kind; the sly spying software kind. Cookies are small programs which the site uses to write a text file to visitors' machines. Cookies may also collect information about site visitors without the visitors' knowledge. All the large sites use them to gather information about visitors for their marketing department. To be fair, some cookies are useful. They store information about a visitor, so that the visitor doesn't have to repeatedly enter the same information, such as an e-mail address, or a password. Many Internet users are wary of cookies, so if you intend using them, put a notice somewhere on the site about your reason for using them.

- **Java and Javascript.** Java is a programming language which creates nifty little software applications. Some of them are useful: they might run video files when the site loads. Others, such as animated graphics, have no useful purpose other than to draw attention to material on the site. However, there are many problems with using Java on your site. The major problem is that you're trimming the size of your audience. Many of your visitors won't have a Java-enabled browser—Java only runs on 32-bit machines. Those who do will often be behind a firewall—this is network hardware and software which limits access to and from the Internet from an internal network or computer, for security reasons. Java is not compatible with firewalls. The upshot of this is that the viewer is confronted with a series of security violation errors, and will (rightly) blame you and your site for the error messages.

- **Audio clips, video clips.** Great stuff, but use them in moderation. Don't use them at all if you have no pressing reason to do so, such as demonstrating something that you're selling. If you do opt for them, don't force your visitors to load the audio or video file the moment they reach your site. Many viewers won't have the necessary plug-ins for multimedia files, or they may not want to wait for the file to load—viewers are usually in a hurry. Of course, you can have multimedia on your site. Just be sure to present it as a file which the viewer can choose to download, or not. For example, if you're selling cars, and you have a video tour of the latest model, provide it as a downloadable presentation (in several formats) which viewers can download and view at their leisure.

General Web page design tips

- Integrate the site. When a viewer visits your site, they're subconsciously looking for a sense that the site is a single entity, so the first impression should be one of integration. Put your logo on every page of the site, and place a link back to your home page on every page, so that the viewer knows where they are at all times. You should also include an e-mail link on every page.
- Watch the colour combinations you use, and aim for good contrast. The best sites use pale colours, or white, for the background, with sharp black type for text. A dark background with white or coloured type is hard to read, so avoid it. Don't use a photograph as a background, as the text melts into the photo. A computer monitor

isn't a sheet of paper, and many people who visit your site will have less than perfect vision, so don't make your site hard to view.

- Present your information logically. Visitors to your site are there for a reason. They should be able to find the information they want immediately. Include an index or a menu if your site has lots of information.

- Break up slabs of text. If you're presenting a full page of undifferentiated text, reduce the column size to half. This is because the eye can cover a line of type of this length at a glance.

- Provide internal links so that the viewer doesn't need to scroll down the screen. Many viewers rest their hand on the mouse and simply click. If the information they want is at the bottom of a page, they may not see it. If your page is wide in a particular browser, work to redesign the page so that viewers don't have to scroll across.

- Use graphics, but keep them small in file size—under 30Kb. Dense, text-filled pages are unappealing, but if you're providing graphics, they should be there for a reason and shouldn't be purely ornamental. Provide a mix of icons, larger graphics and text.

CREATE A BLUEPRINT FOR BUILDING YOUR ONLINE BUSINESS

Now your site is online, you can create an online marketing plan. Unless you're looking for funding from a bank or other source, this doesn't have to be professionally done, nor should it be boring and rigid—it's primarily for your own use and the use of your staff. You can create your blueprint for building your online business on the back of a large envelope, or on a piece of cardboard. Keep it casual—if it's casual, you won't feel bad when you change it. You should look at your plan every week, and feel comfortable changing it as you obtain new information. The following are items you should include in your blueprint for building your business online.

Your online marketing plan

To build your online business successfully, you need an online marketing plan. This plan should be part of your overall marketing plan: you need to know how much you can afford to invest in your online strategy.

Check that your Web site has:

- A clear statement of the purpose of the business.
- A clear statement of products and services offered.
- A unique feature—what's different about this business?
- Statements of the benefits the visitor can expect from the products and services.
- Credentials and referrals—who knows you? Who trusts you?
- A call to action—what action do you want the prospective customer to take?
- Quick load time: 30 seconds or less.
- Graphics which serve a real purpose.
- Clear backgrounds, easy to read fonts.
- Structured content.
- Useful information.
- Links to other sites.
- The option to return to the home page on each page.
- Clearly stated contact information on each page.
- No spelling or grammatical errors.
- A feedback form.
- Regular updates.

Here's an outline of information you should consider including in your online marketing strategy:

- A one-paragraph summary, detailing the purpose and benefits of your online business.
- A description of your target markets. Remember that online you can slice your niche markets as thinly as you wish.
- A list of online marketing methods you'll employ: a Web site, a newsletter, banner advertising on major search engine sites, e-mailed updates to people who've requested them, etc.
- Include a paragraph on the image of your company that you want to project.
- Your budget. How will you finance site maintenance, and site expansion? Express your budget as a percentage of your projected gross revenues.

Research your plan

Do your market research on the Web itself. Start by looking at your competitors. How many other companies in your industry have an online site? Don't just check out each site once, check the sites over a month or two. Make inquiries, as if you were a customer. How responsive are they to their customers? Who are they trying to attract? What features do they have which might be effective for you?

You should also research your customers. Who buys your product or service? How old are they? Male or female? Average income? How often do they buy, and how often do they buy on the Web? Preferred method of payment? What's your best method of reaching these people and attracting them to your site?

Most of this information is easy to get; you simply need to be alert to your competitors' Web sites. In addition, many companies conduct surveys on the Web, and post the results; check out the business sections of online newspapers and magazines for free market research information.

YOUR WEB SITE AND THE SEARCH ENGINES

One of the ways your potential customers will reach your site is via one of the major search engines. Several of the people I spoke to, including Greg Bacia, said they rely on the search engines and on offline promotions. However, these lucky people are the exceptions.

When you type 'dog grooming products' or 'fly fishing rods' into a search engine, you realise that you aren't the only person selling that particular kind of product on the Web. You may be one of thousands. Trying to get your URL to come up in the first few pages of query results in a search engine can be an exercise in frustration. At this stage, you may be tempted to give up, and look for other ways to promote your Web site. If you think that there are special techniques involved in getting your URL up the front of a search engine, you're right, and you should keep that in mind.

Col Jones runs Southern Star Web Consulting, and has made a study of Web search engines. He advises companies on how to get top billing. He says that there are several points to consider:

> First, be realistic. When you create a site and submit it to a search engine, if you use generic terms such as *gardens*, *books*, or *collectibles*, you won't come up first. It's important that you think of longer terms which reflect your subject and will draw people to the site. Your page titles and content should also reflect these longer terms, of course.

For example, if you're a florist, and you want to sell flowers online, first check out some other florists' sites on the Web—enter 'flowers' into InfoSeek or Excite and see which sites are listed first. What do these sites have in common? Which words are repeated on each site? In your browser, select View, Source from the menu. This will show you the HTML code of the page. Are any Meta tags used? This should give you some inspiration. You could add the following terms to describe your site: 'roses, arrangements, gift baskets, balloons, virtual bouquets, plants, flower care, exotics'. Make sure that whatever terms you use are reflections of the pages they're used on.

If you're selling books on your site, take a hint from other online booksellers. If you go to the Borders site, for example at URL: www.borders.com, you'll see that Borders mention all the current bestsellers on the front page. They know that their customers will be looking for these books: they'll be entering the titles and authors as search terms in the search engines.

He makes the point that not all Web search engines are created equal:

> There are significant differences, and it's essential that you properly submit your site to each engine. You'll find software programs which claim to handle submissions for you, but because the engines are different, you won't get a good result. It's far better to submit to fewer search engines, and come up in the first couple of pages, than to waste time with submissions which don't work.

Often, many of his clients did not submit any page other than the first page:

> There was a rumour that Yahoo would not accept anything other than the root URL of a Web site, which meant that http://www.companyx.com.au was acceptable, but http://www.companyx.com.au/index wasn't. You should submit *every* page on your site to every search engine. If you count on web crawlers to come along and index the site, that may take months, and they may well miss crucial inside pages.

Frames cause a problem for search engines. 'I've advised several clients to drop frames. You can mitigate the barrier frames created for search engines by giving extra thought to your meta tags, but that takes extra work.' (See below for information on meta tags.)

Configuring your Web page for good search engine placement

When you submit your page to a Web search engine, the search engine will use a software program called a robot to check your site. The robot will examine the site, and will use the information gathered to describe and categorise your site. The robot will look at:

- the page title of each page;
- the page contents;
- meta tags on pages;
- ALT text in the pages' images; and
- keywords.

Let's consider these in detail.

Web page titles

Your page title is vital. Think about your own reactions when you use one of the search engines to search the Web. You look at the titles of all the pages returned, and because you don't have time to visit all the pages, you choose the most likely ones based on their title. Your title must make sense, and it should also be enticing if you can manage it.

In HTML the page title is the text between the </TITLE> and </TITLE> tags. This title will usually appear at the top of your listing, and some search engines use the title to link to your page, rather than the URL. Usually search engines will also index the words in your title, however you shouldn't put keywords in your title. We'll look at how to use keywords below.

Let's look at some page titles. Go online now, and search for a topic. Try searching for *Australia,* using AltaVista. You'll see that many page titles which come up are ambiguous—you have no idea what the pages contain, when you judge solely by the title. Additionally, many pages are listed as having No Title, because the page author forgot to title the page. Your page title is the first way you can attract visitors, so make your titles relevant.

Page contents

Some search engines use abstracts. They look at the first few lines of the page and present these as an abstract to give viewers a summary of the information contained on the page. Therefore, you should make sure that the headings and the first few lines of your pages are descriptive, and contain information that you want presented to your prospective clients. Try to use words that your visitors are searching for in those first few sentences.

Some search engines look at more than the first few sentences:

they index the complete page. AltaVista is such an engine: visit AltaVista to see how this complete page indexing works.

Some people are desperate to get good placement in search engines, so they try to fool the search engines by including large lists of keywords at the bottom of pages: often these keywords are repeated hundreds of times. This is called 'spamdexing'; often the authors of these pages will try to hide the lists of keywords by making the text of these words the same colour as the page background. Other authors put hundreds of keywords in Comment tags within pages, so that they're not visible to people who visit the site.

Do these shenanigans work? No, because the search engines have programs which are clever enough to figure out what's happening, and they not only ignore repetition, but they also punish any repetition which is installed purely to get a good placement. The punishment is to ban the site from the search engine; they may even blacklist the site, and the site's registered owners.

How to create great meta tags

What are meta tags? They're simply keyword descriptions about your site which don't appear in the viewer's browser, but which are visible to search engines and allow them to index your site more easily.

Here's what a meta tag looks like:

<meta name= 'keywords' content= 'health, vitamins, sale, bargain'>

The meta tag consists of three parts. Its identifier: meta, the name= attribute, and the content= attribute

Col Jones gave me some hints which help to take the mystery out of meta tags for you. First, he says that you should develop three core keywords or phrases which describe your site. What does your company do best? What is it known for? The keywords are the strategy that your search engine optimisation is based on. If you can get this right, getting top billing in the search engines becomes much easier. Additionally, the keywords are the only thing that the search engines have in common. All the other variables need to be taken into account on an individual basis with each search engine. When you've selected your core three keywords, select another five to seven keywords as secondary. What other things are important about your company?

Next, you should develop descriptions of your company, in

```
writing[1].htm - Notepad
File  Edit  Search  Help
<html>

<head>
<meta name="description" content="Angela Booth Media professional writing and editing
services.
Creative ideas and custom content for Web sites; content management for
Web sites; general business writing.">
<meta name="GENERATOR" content="Microsoft FrontPage 3.0">
<meta name="keywords" content="Writing Services, Editorial Services, Web site content,
Business Writing,
Creative Ideas, Custom Content, Original, Online Promotion, Newsletters, Public Relations,
Proposals, Copywriting,
Advertising, Content Management">
<title>Writing Services</title>
<style>
<!--
-->{ font-family: Times New Roman, serif; font-size: 10 }
</style>


<meta name="Microsoft Theme" content="blends 100, default"><meta name="Microsoft Border"
content="tl, default"></head>

<body bgcolor="#FFFFFF" text="#000000" link="#FF0000" vlink="#FFCC33"
alink="#0000FF"><!--msnavigation--><table border="0" cellpadding="0" cellspacing="0"
width="100%"><tr><td><!--mstheme--><font face="trebuchet ms, arial, helvetica">

<p align="center"><br>
<img src="_derived/writing.html_cmp_blends100_bnr.gif" width="600" height="60" border="0"
alt="Services"></p>

<p align="center"> </p>
<!--mstheme--></font></td></tr><!--msnavigation--></table><!--msnavigation--><table border="0"
cellpadding="0" cellspacing="0" width="100%"><tr><td valign="top"
width="1%"><!--mstheme--><font face="trebuchet ms, arial, helvetica">

<p><a href="creativi.html">Creativity</a></p>
```

Putting your keywords into the meta tags is one of the chief ways of developing a good ranking in the major search engines. Look at the fifth line from the top—this site has made good use of meta tags.

50 words, in 25 words, and in 10 words. For the 50-word description, use all the primary and secondary keywords. Pare this down to create your 25-word description. Finally, create your 10-word description, which focuses on the three core keywords only. This 10-word description is what you submit to the major search engines, in various configurations, according to the requirements of the particular search engine. This 10-word description is also what you put in your meta tags.

It's in categories, page titles and URLs which use your keywords that your hard work really pays off. Col says:

> Go to the directories, such as Yahoo, and find categories which include your three primary keywords. Retitle your pages, if necessary, to include your keywords. If possible, rename some of your files, so that the URLs also include the keywords. When your description slots easily into the

categories in the major search engines, it's much easier to get a good placement in the directories.

ALT text in images

Graphics have become more important on the Web, and some search engines index IMG tags so that people can search for graphics. For example, InfoSeek does this. Even search engines which don't index images will still read and index the image text to get a clearer idea of what the page is all about.

Good design for Web search engines

I asked Col to provide me with his tips for good design, from the point of view of getting a good billing in the major search engines, and here they are:

- The title of your Web site should sum up the site in three or four words, and ideally these should be the kinds of words that someone would type into a search engine to try to find you. (Ask some of your customers what words they would use to find you, and make a list of these.)
- Key phrases from the home page should be reflected in the meta keywords tags.
- The meta description tag should be a good description of the page; it should be stimulating, as well as reflecting the key phrases.
- The body copy of the content on the home page should reflect the topic. Make it highly relevant. Important keywords and phrases should appear early in the page. While this sounds restrictive, it's also crucial.
- Avoid frames. Frames create an unnecessary barrier to search engines trying to index inside pages.
- The top search engines are AltaVista, Excite, HotBot, InfoSeek, Lycos, WebCrawler and Yahoo, so you should make sure that you're submitted to these. These search engines are important because they're heavily promoted and popular. They're the ones which will bring traffic to your site.
- You should submit to other search engines as you have the time, or if you find that others in your industry are doing so.
- Remember the topical directories. These are proliferating, and you

should submit to the ones created for your industry. If you provide medical products or services, you should strive to be listed in the medical directories, for example.

- Don't submit your site once to the major search engines, and leave it at that. Tweak the phrases and meta tags you use until you start coming up in the engines, and then make adjustments as they're needed. The search engines are vital to a Web site's success, especially if you don't have a lot of money for things like banner advertising, spending the time tinkering is usually well worth the effort. Beware of overkill, however. Col says, 'You can tinker forever. You can get your site up in the listings, and then it's bumped further back. I advise clients to make sure that each page is optimised for terms that people are searching for, and then don't worry too much about it.'

Finally, Col says that one of the problems with the online world is that because things can happen very quickly, our expectations rise. He maintains that:

> Web site owners should be wary of creating unrealistic expectations in their customers. I designed a site for a client who was initially able to get orders out to clients on the same day that they were received. He promoted this fact heavily; it was a major benefit he was offering. Then two of his major suppliers developed problems at more or less the same time, and he wasn't able to fill orders as quickly. He'd built up unrealistic expectations, not only in his customers, but also in himself. He's since trimmed back his own expectations and those of his customers, and commits to getting orders out within 48 hours. But because he's promoted his 24-hour delivery in all the search engines, this is creating ongoing problems for him.

HOW WILL YOU SPREAD THE NEWS ABOUT YOUR SITE?

Registering your site with the major search engines is a good way to promote it, however you can do much more. We'll discuss promoting your site in detail later, but here are some points to keep in mind:

- In all your promotions, emphasise the benefits to your customers. The more benefits you can provide, the more traffic you will attract to your site. No matter how worthy your site, you need to provide some up-front value for your visitors. You can do this by providing useful information, entertainment, or freebies (such as contests), as additional benefits which will encourage traffic to your site.

- Start making a list of ways in which you will get the word out about your site. You should plan to promote your site online, as well as offline. You can: scout out other sites which will provide links to your site, and decide which newsgroups you will use to announce your site in Usenet. You can also promote offline: have your site's URL printed on your traditional advertising material, such as on your brochures, flyers and business cards—don't forget to include your URL in your next Yellow Pages ad.
- The major search engines receive millions of hits per day. You need to register your URL with them right away. Then test out the URL. Type in some keywords. Does your site come up?

YOUR SITE AND THE OFFLINE WORLD

Advertising on your site may be an attractive option to other businesses in your local area. Creating a home page for your business on the Internet is a little more complex than ringing the Yellow Pages and placing an ad. Therefore, you may be one of the first businesses in your local area to take your business online. If your site is in any way successful, this can make advertising on your site attractive to others who don't want to go to the bother of developing their own Web site.

Stefan Ruddik is based in Hong Kong, and runs an information site for companies which want to start doing business in Asia. His site contains some 3000 pages, and at last count had around 4000 links. He's proud of his site. 'We've become a gateway to Asia. If you want to start doing business in Asia, then you come to our site. We're sure to have information which will help you.'

The site's revenues are 100 per cent advertising driven:

> I have four salespeople who go out cold calling. Most of the people who visit our site are from the US. The local companies which advertise on our site usually haven't advertised on the Internet before. It's a new experience for them. They want to attract US business, and of course this is more important than ever since the economic downturn in Asia.

We have around 200 000 visitors to our site a month, so advertising on our site is attractive to lots of small companies.

Stefan started his Web site as a hobby while working for an insurance company. Within six months, he was so busy that he had to quit his day job. He believes that the major part of his success is due to the fact that he uses traditional sales techniques. 'I hire people to sell space on the site. They're professional salespeople, and I pay them a commission of 30 to 50 per cent for the space they sell. They know little about the Internet, and not much about computers, but they know the benefits of advertising. They know people.'

Although you may not want to create a site which focuses too heavily on advertising for other businesses, advertising is an integral part of any Web site. Start looking into options now. Offering advertising on your site is one way of trimming the costs.

As you can see, you can't simply create your site, and then forget it. Working on your site is an ongoing process, because you can't possibly do everything that you could do immediately, or even within a month. The most important thing to remember is that you should encourage feedback from your visitors, and put their comments into action. In the next chapter, we'll discuss online marketing in detail.

Marketing on the Internet

Marketing on the Internet is both easier and faster than it is in the offline world. This can be a problem, and it pays to be aware of it. Woody Leonhard struck this 'fast response to online marketing efforts' syndrome in late 1998. Woody is the successful author of many computer books, and with Pete Deegan, the owner of My Computer Company in Sydney, sends out a free weekly Internet e-mail newsletter called 'Woody's Office Watch'—WOW for short. WOW has around 40 000 subscribers. Woody and Pete decided to create a new free e-mail newsletter called 'Woody's Windows Watch', or WWW. They advertised WWW in one of the weekly issues of WOW, with instructions on how to join. The subscribers to WOW thought WWW was something they'd like to find in their e-mail box, and tried to join WWW en masse within hours of the pertinent issue of WOW going out across the world. Unfortunately, Woody and Pete hadn't thought to inform their ISP that they might have thousands of people accessing their Web site within the space of a few hours, and the ISP, spotting all this activity on their servers, thought it was under attack. It shut down Woody and Pete's Web sites. It took Woody and Pete days to get the mess sorted out, and to get online again. While they were offline, people continued to try to subscribe to WWW and, of course, were frustrated when they couldn't do so.

The moral of this story is: when you market online, be prepared for a big, *fast* response from your target market. How can you be prepared?

- Warn your ISP if you expect thousands of visits to your site within a few hours.
- If you're selling an item, make sure you have enough stock.
- Inform your staff of what's happening.

If you've made a success of marketing offline, you'll make a success of it online. If you've been worried about your previously unsuccessful marketing efforts, it's probably because you're not clear on what marketing actually is. This isn't theory: if you understand how marketing works, then you'll be able to do it efficiently for your business. Therefore, in this chapter we discuss marketing in general, and then marketing specifics for the Internet, including making good use of areas such as banner advertising, discussion lists, Usenet, and so on.

If it seems that there is a lot to learn, there is. The Internet requires that you understand broad areas, and how you may be able to use them for your business. Then you'll focus in, and decide on which ones to try.

WHY IS MARKETING IMPORTANT?

Marketing is not selling, rather it's a way of thinking about your business. Marketing's core concept suggests that you don't manufacture a product or create a service and then try to sell it; instead you produce what your clients need. When you produce what your clients need, you have a guaranteed sale. This means that you need to spend most of your energy on research—finding out precisely what your clients want and need. In fact, you could build a case that marketing is nothing more than research—finding out what your customers want, and then giving it to them.

Many small business people quibble at this. I was at a business breakfast once, and the talk turned to market research. The gentleman sitting beside me became irate. He dismissed the entire marketing concept by saying: 'That's all very well for the corporate sector, but it's just not realistic for the rest of us. Who's got time for research, for goodness sake? Productivity is what's important.'

I wondered why he worried about productivity when he didn't know whether he could sell his goods after he produced them, but I kept my thoughts to myself. I could see his point. Focusing on the customer, finding out what the customer wants, is a hassle. Before the Internet it was also an expensive hassle. However, if you have a Web site, you can do a lot of market research cheaply and painlessly, and good research is the key to effective marketing.

Good market research via your Web site is disarmingly simple. You can do a lot just with e-mail. For example, Edie Davisson, of Edie's Herbals, has a 'MailTo' button (an e-mail link) on the bottom of every page of her Web site. That's all. That's the full extent of her marketing efforts. She says, however, that while it is her only marketing tool, it lets her know exactly what her customers want. Then, of course, she gives it to them. 'They're not shy about telling me what they want,' she says. 'I get an average of fifteen messages every week, and I keep every one of them. They're vital. They let me know which products are working, and which products are not working for my customers. They also point me in the direction in which my business will go over the next few years.'

Edie enters all customer comments and requests received via e-mail into a database:

> Most of the inquiries I get are about how to use specific products. But often they'll include a request, like *I wish you produced your elder lotion in a travel pack.* That was a great idea. So I made up a trio of three products into small bottles with good seals, and packed them in a towelling toilet case. It's now one of our biggest sellers. Every product innovation I've made over the past year has been inspired by a customer.

While marketing means identifying your customers' needs and wants, success in marketing also means meeting those needs more effectively than your competitors, and making sure that your customers know that you do. It can be an effective strategy to put links to your competitors' sites on your own Web site—but make sure that your products really are superior before you decide to do this.

Many small business people think 'promotion' when they think marketing; they should be thinking 'customer needs'. Although we'll talk about the promotions side of marketing later in this chapter, your major marketing efforts should go into finding out what your customers need. When you do that, the other marketing aspects fall into place. The first item on your agenda then, must be to create an *Internet marketing plan*. This is vital. It needn't be complicated—write it on the back of an envelope or on an index card—but do it.

YOUR ONLINE MARKETING STRATEGY— THE FOUR Ps

Marketing your business on the Internet involves the same 'four Ps'—product, price, promotion and place—as it does elsewhere. However, before you get into the four Ps, you should spend some time thinking about your target market. Developing information about your target market is known as market segmentation.

Market segmentation: how well do you know your customer?

Your marketing begins with your customers. How well do you know them? The Internet is a vast, amorphous space. However, sitting at each computer which is connected to the Internet is a person. Your products and services will not appeal to everyone who has an Internet connection. Not everyone with an Internet connection is interested in buying ink jet refills, for example, so not everyone will be looking for inkjetrefills.com, and buying from Justin. You need to find those people who will be interested in the products or services that you're selling—your target market—so that you can market your products to them. Earlier we saw that Woody and Pete got an enormous response to their marketing of WWW. They were using WOW to reach their target market, and the response proved that they knew their customers well.

The first step should be to get a clear sense of your customer. Write down a complete description of your customer, including

> **Simple steps to marketing success**
>
> - Good information = good marketing: make it your mission to learn something new about your customers every day.
> - Be proactive: ask questions, try new things.
> - Get involved: join mailing lists, and contribute.
> - Invest more time than money: spend a few hours each week simply exploring; keep a list of URLs to visit.
> - Share information: learn what you can, and pass the information on. Your willingness to share what you know has an effect. You will become known as a resource, and will earn deserved trust.

income level, job, age, responsibilities (children, mortgage), likes, dislikes, interests—anything you can think of that you know about your customer. If your list is brief, you'll need to find out more about the people you're trying to reach. When you've finished your list, you will know who your target market is—you will have found your market niche.

The primary reason you need to know this data is so that you can find those areas of the Internet (Web sites, newsgroups, mailing lists) which your customers frequent. Then you can post the information about your products and site in these areas. If you're selling baby clothes for example, you will want to post the information in the mailing lists or newsgroups where young mothers can find it, or perhaps you'll want to buy some advertising space on Web sites for parents.

Your products and the prices you charge

The Internet can help you to be more successful in your business because it can:

- Provide focused, inexpensive ongoing market research, which would cost you thousands of dollars if you had to pay for it.
- This research can show you how to add value to your products to help you sell more.
- Build recognition of your business and products.
- Finetune your prices.

These days, a lot of research happens before a product (or service) is created. The product is always designed for a specific market, and hundreds of thousands of dollars may be spent in researching that market. A target market is chosen—say, young women between 25 and 30, and their attitudes, desires and needs are researched thoroughly. Only when the potential customer and her needs have been analysed completely is a product designed.

Additionally, the product is designed as a complete *package*, which consists of the product, the name, the packaging and so on, all designed to appeal to a particular customer. As an example, think of the variety of financial services you can buy at any bank these days. Each banking 'product' has a name which has been selected to appeal to its target market, and the product components also appeal to that market. In a sense, the product has been pre-sold—it has been created solely to satisfy a need of a segment of the market.

With your marketing cap on, you should aim to be on the lookout for new markets, and also for products that you could design to meet the needs of that market: both your current and future customers. You do this by making ongoing marketing research a part of your online business.

Col Jones says most small businesses on the Web fail to do this:

> Finding out about your customers should be your *primary* reason for creating a Web site. Every large business on the Web—Microsoft and Amazon.com to name just two of the best known—focuses on learning more about their customers. They want to know as much as they can about the people who visit their site. If you doubt this, go into your Web browser's Options dialogue, and change the setting so that your browser notifies you when a site places a cookie on your computer. Now go to a large company's Web site—*any* large company of your choice. Your browser will ask you, at least once on every page of the site, whether you want to accept a cookie. You'll get tired of hitting the 'Yes' button. Why all the cookies? Large companies want as much information as they can get on *every* customer. By focusing on promotion, rather than true marketing, small businesses are not making the most of their opportunities on the Web.

Your ongoing market research

The Internet makes market research simple. Within an hour or two, you can collect information about your customers which would have cost you many thousands of dollars to obtain previously. However, the information is useless unless you do something with it. Start by listening to your customers. What do they tell you about your product? What is the most important factor to them? What benefits are they receiving? If you know what benefits your customers perceive as being most important, you can emphasise those benefits.

Greg Bacia believes in database marketing; that is, marketing to a specific list of targeted people. Rather than buying a list, he's created his own. His database was created specifically to store information about the people who live in his area. He says:

> The more you can find out about your clients, the more effectively you can help them. We send out a questionnaire every three months. The

questionnaires go out to those of our clients who are online, as well as via ordinary mail to those who aren't. This is important for us, because our local geographic area is changing. In the past couple of years, five new industrial parks have opened, and the Chamber of Commerce and Industry is trying to draw new businesses into the area. We're getting a lot more young families than we used to. We use the information in our database every day. It means that we can target promotions specifically to certain people; those people who've lived in the area for more than ten years, and who have children, for example—maybe they're looking for a larger home.

Greg says the market research pays for itself. A market research company designs the questionnaires, and also analyses them. 'I don't have the expertise to do that myself,' Greg says. 'Having them professionally done also means that I can sell focused information to other businesses in the area. I send out an informational newsletter as well, which goes to members of our local professional associations.'

Online research downloaded from Web sites of large market research companies adds to the value of the information gathered from the questionnaires sent out. Greg summarises information he's found online for the newsletter. He says that the market research aids his marketing efforts in two ways: 'It's a way of finding clients, and targeting them with promotions, but it also promotes our business—it keeps our company name in front of people.'

Adding value to your products

Value-adding is a buzzword of the nineties. It's a way of differentiating your products and services in a crowded market place, and selling more. A 'value' is a benefit to your customer. If you add value effectively, you will sell more, because you're providing what people want. For example, market research has shown that many young women aged from 20 to 30 don't cook; they buy ready-cooked frozen meals at the supermarket, or they and their families eat out. The large supermarket chains now sell ready-to-cook fresh meals. It's a great way of value-adding to the fresh food they're selling already.

Think about how you can add value to your product. Can you provide a toll-free number? What about insurance? Or service contracts? Gift coupons? Free Christmas and Easter gift wrappings? Your Web site is adding value to your products and services, of course. The

Web site makes it easy to communicate with you and to buy your products, and this is an added value.

Build recognition of your business and product names

You need to build recognition of your business and product names online. The easiest way is by using your business name as your domain name. Obtaining domain names is relatively inexpensive. If you think that you will be developing a new product or service, think about whether you should obtain a domain name now for that new product or service.

If you obtain another domain name, this will let you hive off the product or service for which that domain was acquired. This may be a good idea. Col Jones recommends to his clients that they keep their site simple:

> If you restrict a Web site to a primary concept, it's easy to promote the site in various ways, such as through Web search engines. When you start adding new products and services to the site, it can become unfocused. This confuses your customers. I tell my clients that if they consider a product important, then they should create a site which focuses only on that product.

The prices you charge

If you're aiming to attract customers from outside Australia, visitors to your Web site will expect to see prices quoted in US dollars. If you sell Australian opals, for example, as Alexa Parisi of Gemstone Dreaming does, the bulk of your business will be with overseas clients. Some sites get around the currency difficulty by adding a link to a currency conversion site, but this is distracting. The easiest way around it is to post your prices in both US and Australian dollars.

Alexa Parisi quotes prices in both currencies:

> It can be a hassle when the value of the Australian dollar changes several times over the course of a week. When I first launched the site, I used to change the prices to reflect the changes in the value of the dollar. That was an *enormous* headache. Now I don't bother. Most of my clients want to negotiate the price, they expect to do that.

Currency aside, much of your online pricing tactics depend on what your competitors are doing. You won't want to charge less than others are charging for similar products, unless you're doing it to gain a tactical advantage. If you do decide to price a product low, remember that it should still pay its share of your overheads. Online businesses may have fewer overheads, however you need to make enough profit to be able to reinvest in your business.

You can charge more for a product or service if you feel that you've added sufficient value to a product. Alexa says the secret is to make sure that your products and services are unique, if you can:

> Find out what you can do that is special, and that meets the needs of your customers. For example, I include a choice of free basic settings with each stone, either as a pendant or as a brooch. For collectors who aren't interested in a setting, but in information, I include a full description of each stone, plus data about where the stone was mined, including photographs. If appropriate, I also include information on the gem-cutter who cut and polished the stone, and so on. This is all adding value.

Placing your products

The 'place' aspect of the four Ps involves how your product reaches the customer—that is, your distribution network.

Your Web site is part of your distribution network—after all, it gives you a global reach. This only applies, however, if people know that the site exists. Making sure that your site is accessible via search engines and subject guides is vital. Exchanging links with other sites is also vital. The more links you can create to your site, the more your site traffic will be boosted. In one sense, creating as many paths to your site as possible is the online version of a distribution network.

Promoting

Promoting your business online is a public relations exercise. It means letting your customers know that you've created products which they want and need. When you take your business online, you will be focusing on online promotions. However, your offline promotions— the way you promote your business now, in traditional media, such as Yellow Pages ads, classified ads in newspapers, display ads in local newspapers, etc—are still important. Don't neglect your offline promotions in favour of online. Remember that it will take at least a year for your business to flourish online. (See 'The business cycle on the Internet—keep marketing!' on page 87 for more information.)

Consider both offline and online promotions. The major forms of promotion are:

- Advertising. You can advertise in conventional media, such as newspaper or magazine ads, to promote your online business. You can also advertise online—via banner ads and more. We cover these online promotions later in this chapter.
- Special sales promotions. Contests, giveaways, a percentage off the price, and so on. You will need to promote these promotions both offline and online.
- Public relations efforts. This involves speeches, news releases, newsletters, sponsorship of events or worthy causes, etc. Your Web site and every e-mail message you send are also part of your public relations efforts.
- Presentations. Again, both online and offline. These presentations may be to prospective buyers, or to salespeople or agents.

We'll go into more detail on promotions later in the book, because this is an important aspect of taking your business online.

Think direct marketing

Jenny Firestone, of public relations company Firestone & Wallace PR, believes that marketing on the Web is similar to direct marketing:

> I worked as a copywriter preparing many direct marketing campaigns, and the Web is a similar situation. I hear complaints that people don't want to buy via the Web, but if you go and check out the complainer's Web site it becomes obvious why visitors don't buy. A Web site should generate an immediate response from the prospective customer, that is, from the visitors to the site.

Here are Jenny's tips:

1. When I was writing direct marketing letters, I learned that you should focus on results. You must be clear about what you want the viewer to do, and you must say so. This means that you need to be clear in your own mind. Do you want people to buy a product immediately? Are you trying to build leads to future sales?

Are you building up a mailing list for your print catalogue? Or do you want to conduct research?

2. Only when you know what you want will you be able to build up an offering and develop the key selling points—the benefits to your customer. Always put yourself in the customer's shoes. What benefits are you offering in return for a response? You could be offering products at 30 per cent less than similar products sell for in retail stores; this is a great benefit. If you're conducting research, you could offer prizes in return for the time people spend filling out your questionnaire—this is also a benefit. Focus on the benefit. Tell people what they will get out of it. Don't hint at what the benefit will be—describe the benefit in plain language. Make sure that you preview anything that you put on your Web site. Ask someone who doesn't know your business intimately whether they can immediately see what the benefit is to the customer.

3. You should also put your order form, or the request for the viewer's name and address, right on your home page. If they like your offer—*buy one of our videos, get another one free*—they shouldn't have to hunt for the form to fill in. In fact, if they do have to hunt for it, you will probably lose them.

Think free!

Successful businesses on the Web give something away. This draws visitors to the site. Out of all those visitors come your buyers, just through sheer force of numbers.

Barbara Adams created her first Web site in 1996, and this made her aware of the power of the freebie. She had just been downsized out of a job, and was looking around for something she could do. She created a site for a friend, a travel agent:

> Giving something away was an afterthought. I developed the site as a time saver for my friend, because mapping out itineraries for clients took her so much time. The Web site allows clients to create their own itinerary. My idea was to have the site set up so that you could enter the destination, the length of time people wanted to be away, and the amount of money they were prepared to spend. We also wanted to develop our own direct marketing list. For that, we had to give people a reason for giving us their names and addresses, and some details about themselves. So we gave out a prize every month.

No one was more surprised than Barbara when the site was a huge success, resulting in a 30 per cent increase in bookings. 'Once a month, we gave away a weekend for two on the Gold Coast. People could enter as many times as they liked, and they could take the prize whenever it suited them.'

Barbara is convinced that the prizes drew customers to the site. 'When they stopped the prizes for three months, the number of visitors dropped, and the bookings dropped as well.'

You don't have to give prizes to draw people to your site. The Internet is about information, so that can be your freebie. If you provide information that people find valuable, you'll draw people to your site.

THE BUSINESS CYCLE ON THE INTERNET—KEEP MARKETING!

Your online marketing activities are no different from your other marketing activities—you need to pursue them consistently. Although time seems compressed in online transactions because they happen much more quickly, a business still requires around the same amount of time to become established in cyberspace as it does in the 'real' world.

Edie Davisson estimates that it took around six months before her online sales became significant. 'You need to keep marketing, keep promoting your current products, and creating new ones.' Edie believes that business owners should not expect results from the online area of their business for at least twelve months. 'If it happens sooner, it's a nice surprise, but you shouldn't count too much on it. This is why a lot of small business people became disillusioned with the Web. They were bedazzled by the potential of the market, and they forgot the basics of business, which are the same everywhere.'

If you've run other businesses, you know that your business will take around twelve months to get on its feet. During that twelve months, marketing is a key activity, and it should remain a key activity as long as you are in business. With any new business, at around nine months, online or off, there's a definite danger period. Sales trickle off or plateau at a certain level, and bills start coming in faster than receivables, which may slow down. This is the stage at which business owners who haven't been through this cycle before tend to panic.

It's vital that you expect this to happen. Expect a slowdown in your online business, during the first nine to twelve months. It's a cycle. If you think that this cycle is a permanent state of affairs, you may close your business down just before you make a breakthrough. Edie says:

> Time and again, on business-related mailing lists, you can watch this happening to others. It happened to me. The key is to hang in, and *keep marketing*. You've got to be consistent in marketing. Your market research will expand your product line, and your marketing promotions will attract new customers—it will also remind people who've heard of you that you still exist.

This is why it's vital that you pay attention to your offline business activities even as you develop the online portion. Don't stop your offline promotions just because you've taken your business online. Your offline and online activities should work together.

Another thing to be aware of as your online business goes through its cycles is that the Internet has slow periods as well. Slowdowns occur during the major holiday periods. The biggest slowdown is at Christmas. Even in the northern hemisphere, where business picks up in September after the northern summer, business drops off sharply after 1 December, and doesn't pick up again until after the first week of January. Of course, the same thing happens in Australian business at this time, because as well as Christmas we have the major school and work summer holiday periods in December–January. So when you begin making online contacts, and conducting business with people on the other side of the world, expect the Christmas period to be slow. You won't get as many visits to your Web site. Take this opportunity to make major changes or overhauls to your site if you wish. If not, there's no harm in joining the rest of the world and taking a break.

Easter is another slow period on the Internet. The northern summer period of June through August is also sluggish, and if you trade internationally, take this into account.

The key to managing these cycles effectively is to keep up your marketing right through them. When you create your marketing plan, take both the cycles of your own business and the greater cycles of the Internet into account. And keep marketing—both offline and online.

Create a marketing plan—and stick to it

Edie Davisson believes that when you take your business online a marketing plan is vital. Her advice is to keep your plan current. 'You can revise this plan as often as you wish, but don't tinker with it too much. If money starts flowing into the business very quickly, don't spend it all on expansion. Set a portion aside for the slower times, when not as much money comes in, but you still need to pay your bills.'

Your marketing plan will be as individual as your business. It can include:

- New products and services you want to develop.
- Specific promotions you intend to undertake, and where (Web site, newsgroups, mailing lists, classifieds, banner advertising).
- Follow-ups and evaluations of your promotions—did they work?
- Budgeting time and money for the above.
- Specific deadlines—these are vital. You need to ground your plan in reality by assigning dates to activities.

EFFECTIVE ONLINE MARKETING

All marketing begins with research. Once your Web site is up, you can interact with visitors to the site and turn them into customers by providing what they want and need.

Chatting to your customers on the Web

Your presence at your business is a strong marketing tool. You need to be there, and you need to talk to your potential customers. Some business owners who depend heavily on personal contact are wary of the Internet, because it seems so impersonal. They feel threatened. How can they know what will work when they no longer have contact with customers? They're always amazed to find that their online relationships with customers can be even stronger than their relationships with customers who come into their store or office. This is because people will tend to tell you the truth online—if you ask them. Perhaps this is because the online world is partially anonymous. You may know someone's name and the company they work for, but you can't *see* them.

Personal contact with visitors to your site is important, and yes,

Chat software for your Web site is available at many locations on the Internet. Try ZDNet at www.zdnet.com, or just type 'chat software' into one of the search engines. You can also try these URLs for companies offering free chat programs and world pagers:

http://www.parachat.com

http://www.mirabilis.com

http://www.voxware.com—with this program, you can even conduct online conferences, vital if the majority of your sales are in the business-to-business area.

you can talk to your potential customers as they browse your site. You do this via 'chat' software. You may be aware of the section of the Internet called Internet Relay Chat—IRC. IRC is similar to Usenet (the online discussion groups), but on IRC the chats take place in real time. It's a slow way of having a conversation, but it appeals to many people.

The people who use chat software on their Web site for interactivity with their customers report that many more people contact them through online chats than ever bother clicking the e-mail button. The immediacy of the response is appealing. However, chat software isn't for everyone. It means that you need to spend a lot of time at your computer, so it only works for those businesses where you tend to spend a lot of time in your office. If you do decide to try chat software, set a time frame for when you will be online for visitors to chat to you, and post the times on your site. If many of your site visitors are from overseas, then post your availablility in their local times.

A very effective marketing tactic is to host online chat events at your site with a celebrity, or with someone well known in your industry. You can advertise these events in newsgroups, mailing lists, and of course on your Web site. When the event is over, edit the transcript, and archive it on your site for future visitors to see.

An alternative to chats is a Message Board area. You can post a FAQ (frequently asked questions) page in this area, as well as announcements on sales and specials. The software you use to create message boards allows the messages to be threaded, meaning that posts are organised by topic, and then chronologically. By doing this, you can create a sense of community, allowing your customers to talk to each other as well as to you. To find message board software, enter 'message board software' into one of the search engines, or go to ZDNet's software archive at www.hotfiles.com.

Auto e-mail with autoresponders

If you've ever sent a message to an e-mail address, and had a reply in your mailbox seconds later, you may wonder how the company did that. They did it by using an autoresponder, and you can too. In fact, if you have more than ten e-mail messages a day which want more information about a product or service on your Web site, an autoresponder is a necessity. Autoresponders are programs which send automatic replies when someone sends e-mail to an address linked to your site. You can use an autoresponder to send further information, advise of updates to your site, send out e-mail newsletters, and much more. The chief benefit of using an autoresponder is the time it saves you in dealing with e-mail. The easiest way to add this automatic feature to your Web site is to have your ISP set it up for you. This service isn't expensive. Most ISPs charge around $15 to set up an autoresponder, and then add around $5 a month to your account to pay for the service.

If your ISP won't install an autoresponder for you, you can buy autoresponders online. The easiest way to learn about autoresponders, and how you can use them in your business, is to trial one. Some companies offer mini versions free. Try:

EXCITEMAIL at http://www.excite.com
BIGFOOT at http://www.bigfoot.com

The free programs available at these two sites won't let you send lengthy messages, but they do give you a taste of what this kind of software can do. When your Web site is up, and if you receive lots of inquiries, your autoresponder could save you hours of work each day.

Edie Davisson has an autoresponder on her site:

Before I got it, I had a couple of canned responses which I sent out to people who inquired. But that meant cutting and pasting from informational files on my computer, and each reply took a couple of minutes—if I got fifteen requests, they took me half an hour to answer. The autoresponder saves me a lot of time, so I've devoted more time to creating additional material. For example, I have an online brochure that I send out to people who ask for it via the autoresponder. I just selected a few paragraphs from my printed materials, and edited them so that they are more conversational. There's also a *Who are we?* section in the online brochure, which I think is important. People like to know who they're doing business with.

Greg Bacia uses an autoresponder to send out online news releases:

I don't just send them to media outlets or to online newsletters who might be interested in what we do. I send them out—or the autoresponder does—to everyone on my e-mail contacts list. I worried about doing that at first, since people hadn't asked specifically to receive it. But I explained how to remove yourself from the mailing list at the end of the message. They go out around once a month.

MARKETING PROMOTION—ADVERTISING ON THE WEB

It seems there's no end to the various forms of advertising on the Web. The following is a basic selection to get you started. Keep in mind that when viewers are browsing the Web they're in a certain frame of mind. They're not sitting in a lounge chair, or relaxed in front of the television. They're not even as relaxed as they would be if they were reading a magazine. They're sitting in an upright chair, usually at work, using a machine which was designed for the work environment. This work-oriented frame of mind of the majority of Web surfers is borne out when you look at the top-rating sites. The search engines always rate ahead of any other sites. Therefore, when you advertise on the Web, keep the orientation of Web surfers in mind. They're at work. They're busy. You can be your own guinea pig too—watch your own reactions to advertising on the Web: what attracts you in an advertising banner? What derails you from your purpose, and makes you click to a site you had no intention of visiting? When this happens, think about what made you go to the site.

Classifieds

It's easy to overlook this basic form of advertising, but it can be effective. Try the Online Trading Post (URL: http://www.tradingpost.com.au) to see whether it has potential for you. Classifieds can work in many kinds of businesses, and they're a good, cheap addition to your Internet marketing plan. Take the time to investigate all the sites offering classifieds, both in Australia and, if your products travel, overseas. Some of these classifieds are free; the Web sites which provide them make money from selling advertising on their sites.

Paid listings

These are offered on large sites which function as industry directories. The site puts up pages of links, categorised in various ways. Companies pay a once-off or monthly fee to be listed on the page, so you can think of it as being similar to the Yellow Pages. The listing contains the company's (or individual's) name, their URL if they have a site, their e-mail address, company address, and also phone and fax numbers. These paid listings are useful in the same way that local area Yellow Pages directories are useful. If someone in your local area is looking

Visit the eMarketer site to get started advertising on the Web. The site provides statistics and information about Internet advertising and marketing.

for a Shiatsu practitioner, or a desktop publisher, then the paid listing directs them to you. Before you pay for such a listing, however, check out how the site is indexed on the major search engines. You're looking for all the pages on the site to be indexed, because you want your name to come up if someone does a search for 'Shiatsu Greendale NSW', for example.

Banner advertising

Banner ads are those thin advertising ribbons (usually 600 pixels wide and 40 pixels high) which show up everywhere you go on the Web. They're colourful, and often animated. They usually load before the information loads, so your potential customers have a few seconds to study your message. The keywords in banner advertising are provocative and informative—remember that the viewers have a purpose, they're working. It takes a real jolt to shake them out of that work mindset, and to get them to click to your site. You can buy banner ad space on other sites, and you can sell banner ads on your own site to anyone who may want to advertise there. And if your site becomes wildly popular, others will want to advertise on it. Outside advertising can become a vital revenue stream for you. This is why it's important that you devote time to your site, and keep it updated.

The main thing to remember about your banners (and about your Web site in general) is to keep file sizes small. We're not talking about viewing size, but about how long a file takes to download. When someone visits your site, what actually happens is that your site is visiting them: it's being copied to their machine, byte by byte. Between the time the viewer clicks on your banner ad, and your home page appears on their machine, all kinds of things are happening in the background, any of which can slow down the display of that page. You don't want to know how it all happens, all you need to know is that if you ask people to visit your site, and it consists of huge files, they're going to go somewhere else where they don't have time to make a phone call and drink a cup of coffee before the page loads onto their machine.

Sponsorships

There are many kinds of sponsorships on the Web. Your choice will definitely be limited by your budget. Sponsorships are usually available on content Web sites. That is, newspapers, magazines, and so on. In addition, they're available on games sites, kids' sites, sites for women—in other words, sites offering information for special interest groups. Why bother with a sponsorship? The keyword is commitment. When a site advertises 'brought to you by', and displays your clickable logo, you're linked with that site in the viewer's mind. It gives you prestige—if the site is well known—and credibility.

If you have a high budget, the sky is the limit in sponsorships. You can sponsor a site in any worthy area that you choose. You can choose a site that has prestige value, or a site which is fun for viewers, or a reference site. For a SOHO operator with a low budget, the most important sponsorships are those of newsletters and mailing lists. You can, of course, also sponsor an entire site. The good part about sponsorships is that you simply pay the money, and in return you get a 'brought to you by' heading, with your URL and other info, on the newsletter or mailing list. You don't have to worry about the time involved in creating the newsletter, or maintaining the mailing list.

Letting others advertise on your site

If you're gathering thousands of hits a day, others will start wanting to share in some of that traffic. Even if you're not generating a lot of hits, you may receive inquiries about site advertising from companies whose business complements yours—for example, if you're selling boutique wines, you may get an inquiry from a large winery that wants to advertise on your site.

Web advertising is usually charged by the number of impressions, that is, views of the ad. Currently, $30 per 1000 views seems to be an average rate for larger sites. Smaller sites charge anywhere from $5 to $30 per 1000 views. However, if your site is well targeted at a special demographic which another company wants to reach, then you can charge a lot more. Some sites reputedly have charged $1 an impression. If you want to get an idea of what you could charge for advertising on your site, your best bet is to visit some sites which are similar to yours and find out how much they charge. Often sites will display an advertising rate card; if they don't, then check out the IPA Advertising Index at URL: http://www.netcreations.com/ipa/adindex/#search. This takes you to the search form, but you can choose the List option to browse through the database.

The Online Advertising Mailing List

It's worthwhile joining this mailing list, because you'll get a frank discussion of what advertisers are paying, and what Web sites are charging —which is often a lot different from what their rate card would have you believe. The URL for the online form to subscribe to the list is: www.tenagra.com/online-ads.

You probably won't find your chief competitors' rates, but you can click on various sites of different sizes to see how much they're charging, and what their pricing structure is like. When you've found several sites which appear similar to your own, visit the sites and see how much advertising they've managed to attract. You could also check to see whether they've raised their rates from the rate in the database by checking the rate card. But what if they don't have any advertising? It could be that they haven't promoted the site effectively, or perhaps they haven't gone out to win advertising dollars.

Selling ad space on your site

The first step when you want to sell ad space is to create a rate card. Don't price yourself out of the market by making the advertising on your site much more expensive than the rates charged on similar sites. Then place your rate card on the site, with a MailTo button.

There's a problem if your site is very new, because you won't have a long site-flow history. In this situation, try offering space at a flat-rate fee for three months. This means that the advertiser isn't losing, and they may have clinched a bargain if your site becomes a roaring success in that time.

You could also consider giving someone free advertising on your site for a few weeks—to prime the pump, so to speak. Other advertisers may be more inclined to place an ad if it seems as if someone else has already done so.

You track the traffic to your site via your ISP's logging system. When you're ready to start selling advertising space on your site, get in touch with the marketing department of your ISP to find out how this works.

Selling in cyberspace

In this chapter, we'll cover electronic commerce—what it takes to make sales on the Internet, including the vital matter of price points, and how you'll accept payment for your goods and services. We'll also look into projecting future sales on your Web site, and how you can boost those sales.

Scams on the Internet attract a lot of media attention, and we'll look at some common scams later in this chapter. However, although Internet security (or the lack thereof) and scams get a lot of offline publicity, you shouldn't allow yourself to become paranoid. The reason scams attract attention is because they are so unusual—most folk you find online are generous with their time and their expertise, and are scrupulous in their business dealings. I communicated with dozens of business people as I prepared this book, and none I spoke to had ever been the victim of an online scam.

Finally, we'll deal with some legitimate and illegitimate sales tactics on the Internet.

INTERNET SALES IN A NUTSHELL

Here's a brief summary of how to start making sales on the Internet.

1. Decide what you want to sell.
2. Develop your Web site. Strictly speaking, you don't really need a Web site to make Internet sales. You can use Internet classifieds,

banner advertising and e-mail mailing lists to get your products and services known. However, the people who hear of your products online will want to visit your Web page. It gives you credibility. You could even link a personal home page to your business Web page so that customers can learn more about you. Your online customers want to know that they are dealing with a real person. Think about including a photo of yourself, your staff and your business premises somewhere on the site.

3. Advertise your Web site as much as you can. If nothing else, submit your site to the Internet search engines. If possible, also contribute to Internet discussion groups such as Usenet, and mailing lists, using your signature file. A 'sig' file is the small block of text at the end of an e-mail message or a newsgroup posting which says something about the person who sent the message, or perhaps something the person wants other people to know. This is another way for your name to cross the computer screens of your current and potential customers.

4. Obtain autoresponder software to automate sending out e-mail information files about your business.

ELECTRONIC COMMERCE

E-commerce? Selling things from a Web site? If you're selling products via your Web site, your aim should be to make the sales as automated as possible. A good way to start is with 'shopping cart' software. This needn't be expensive. If you're suspicious of this, there's no need to be. It should be your aim to have your Web site do as much work as possible for you. Perhaps you've been thinking of a Web site as something like an electronic billboard. You can use it in this way of course, but with a little extra effort your Web site can do much more. Even if you don't want to use full-blown e-commerce options, you should aim for some client interaction on your site. It can be simple. For example, you could offer:

- A form in which the viewer can register for something: product updates, a newsletter, etc.
- A feedback form, to gather information: find out what they like about your products, and what they don't like.
- Classified ads: if you sell office equipment, you could offer free classifieds for your customers to sell their used equipment.

Electronic commerce: CyberCash offers real-time online credit card payments.

As you can see, the options on the kinds of simple interaction on your site, which help you to sell, are limited only by your needs, and by your imagination.

However, you should aim for complete interaction, and that means making sales online. If you're thinking, 'Yes, but I sell equipment worth thousands of dollars—how can I make online sales?', consider this: McGrath & Partners, a Sydney real estate company, conducted an online auction of a property in March 1998. The auction was completely interactive: viewers could bid online while the auction went on. Even though the property wasn't sold to an online bidder, it showed that the technology was available to do it. Although McGrath & Partners are not making online auctions a feature of their site yet, other real estate firms have indicated that they will soon be doing so.

As of mid-1998, there are no standards for digital commerce on the Internet, but companies such as Microsoft and IBM are working on creating standards for SET (Secure Electronic Transactions). This makes selling in cyberspace currently a freewheeling proposition. The most common kinds of transactions use credit cards and cheques. Companies such as CyberCash have developed systems for putting paper dollars onto the Internet, by storing credit card information on the user's PC. However, few users are signed up for the system. Ecash is another new system. It's a form of cyber money developed by DigiCash. Using the Ecash program, a user withdraws money from their bank, and stores it as digital dollars on their own PC.

Since there are no standards, be guided by your bank, your credit card company, and whoever is hosting your site. If you intend accepting online credit card payments, your site host's server computers have to be set up to maintain security. This means that information such as credit card details are sent encrypted, so that the packets of information cannot be intercepted by a third party. However, no matter how secure you think your online security is, some people will never be happy sending their credit card details across the Net. You need to provide other options. Alternatives to a secure server include:

- Asking your customers to call you with their credit card information.
- Asking them to fax you card details.
- Having them send the card information via two separate e-mail messages.

Some of your customers won't want to send you their credit card information at all, and will want to send you a cheque. Make sure that your international clients send bank drafts in Australian funds. If the goods or services you sell are high priced, you may want to look into electronic bank transfers. Electronic commerce is so new that site owners are doing what works for their customers—which is the way it should be, after all.

E-commerce software

Most e-commerce development software which is targeted at small business costs from $5000–$10 000. These programs include templates for online catalogues and databases. This makes it easy to change products and prices from day to day. They also include search facilities, which are dynamic—that is, they will offer different information when an item is out of stock or on special. The search facility can also be integrated with existing back-end systems for order fulfilment, as well as a range of automatic payment options. If you're interested in one of these programs, it's advisable to have your Web site designer, or a software consultant, set it up and program it for you, so that it integrates efficiently with all the other software you use in your business.

It's easy to locate e-commerce programs on the Web. Any of the search engines (Excite, AltaVista) will give you a listing. Currently available programs which are suitable for small business include:

- Net.Commerce Suite from IBM
- Electronic Commerce Suite from iCat
- Online from Intershop
- CatSmart from Isadra
- WebCatalog and WebMerchant from Pacific Coast Software
- Cat@log from The Vision Factory
- Domino.Merchant from Lotus

Price points on the Web

Pricing is a very hot topic among business people on the Web. Here's a checklist that may ensure that your pricing falls within acceptable limits for your clients—and which allows you to make enough money to stay in business:

1. Is your price comparable to what the consumer would expect to pay if they shopped offline? Web buyers are resistant to paying 5 per cent to 10 per cent more for products on the Web (excluding shipping) unless you can point to

Reality Check: can you make billions via e-commerce?

The short answer is no, not unless you're dealing in the business-to-business market. The US investment bank Piper Jaffray estimates that in 2001, $US228 billion will be transacted over the Internet, but only 11 per cent of that will be in retail sales. As of mid-1998, no retail business model has been devised to ensure that your business will make more money online than offline. However, that doesn't mean that you can ignore the online world. The Internet is delivering on its promise as an information medium, which means that more and more people are researching their purchases online, even though they will probably buy from a physical retail store. You need an online presence to disseminate information quickly and easily.

clear service advantages or added value. In fact, since you are saving money using the Internet, you should aim to pass on some of these savings to your clients. Make it clear what your offline prices are, and what savings your customers can make by ordering online.

2. Do your prices compare favourably with the prices of other companies in your industry? Remember, it's easy to find out what others are charging online.

3. Do your prices look as though they are based on your cost, or do they look contrived, as if you're aiming for a specific retail pricing point, such as $549, or $299? Round off your prices—to $550 or $300 in the above examples. Keep the maths simple.

HOW TO BOOST YOUR INTERNET SALES

You can boost your Internet sales in a number of ways:

- By using direct mail.
- By designing your Web site to encourage sales.
- By checking on your site's sales-ability via Web site evaluations.
- By demo-ing your site: look on it as a sales tool.
- By participating in newsgroups.
- By creating an online newsletter.
- By putting your product database online.
- By giving something away.
- By using an 'associate' program.
- By submitting your site to search engines, and checking your submissions regularly.
- By passing on your savings to your customers.

Let's look at these options in more detail.

Use direct mail

Use direct mail (through Australia Post) to alert your current clients to your online site. They have to know that your site is online. The most rapid way to build recognition of your site (and to start saving and making money) is to send out a traditional direct mailing to your current customers. If you read 'how we did it' stories published on the Internet or in magazines of Web sites that are doing phenomenally well, direct mail often features somewhere in the equation. Depending on your business, you could find that many of your current customers are online. If they are, they'll appreciate the time and money that ordering over the Internet will save them. Make sure you show your appreciation for their support of your online activities by giving them a reward of some kind.

Design your site to encourage sales

If you have a database of your goods and services, it should be online. That way, not only your customers, but also your staff, can access it easily. While they are on the phone, your staff can say: 'Let me just check that on the Web site . . .' They can then pass out the URL. Not only is this an efficient way for your staff to access the information they need to pass on, but it's also a way of promoting your site. Your database should update itself automatically so that it accurately reflects the goods that you have on hand. Designing such a database is a specialised task, and you'll need to hire someone to do the job for you. Make sure that when your database goes online you know enough about its workings so that you can make minor repairs on it yourself. For more on putting your database online, see page 107.

Check on your site's sales-ability via Web site evaluations

You've built the site and you've had some feedback, but you need more. Evaluating your site should be an ongoing process, because it's your primary online sales tool. Although you can pay for a site evaluation, you can also obtain free evaluations, as well as handy hints on how you can improve your site. Try these options:

- Ask your customers to visit your site and fill in an online questionnaire with their reactions.
- Ask your business contacts—suppliers, distributors—to do the same.
- Join a mailing list, such as I-Sales (Internet Sales URL: http://www.mmgco.com/isales.html). The members of I-Sales swap critiques of each other's sites. The list members are all small business owners with an online presence, and they are very knowledgeable.

Demo your site: it's a sales tool

Take every opportunity you can to demo your site. You can do this at meetings, or at trade shows. At trade shows, there's no need to exhibit—simply call up your site on any monitor at the show which has Internet access. How do people respond to the site? Are they interested, or not? Other options are to call up your site at Internet cafes, on university campuses if you're giving a presentation, whenever you give a presentation for a client—and anywhere else you can find a monitor and an Internet connection.

Gauge the responses you get. As well as being a sales tool, this is another way of gaining evaluations of your site—and boosting sales. After seeing your site navigated by people unfamiliar with it, you may be inspired to overhaul the entire site.

Participate in Usenet newsgroups

Usenet is a collection of online discussion groups, called 'newsgroups'. There are tens of thousands of newsgroups around the globe; around 20 000 are distributed internationally. Newsgroups are devoted to anything you can think of (and to lots of topics you'd probably rather not think of). Whatever you're trying to market or sell, there are many newsgroups with people who are interested. To read newsgroup discussions, you need software called a newsreader. A newsreader comes with your browser; check the Help file to see how to use it. Newsgroups are distributed via Usenet, so you'll see them referred to as simply Usenet, or newsgroups, or Usenet newsgroups.

Participating in Usenet newsgroups will only work if you truly are interested in the area a newsgroup covers. It should be a pleasure for you to share your knowledge. Be sure to include your URL in the sig (signature) line of your posting. The key here is to participate, and to contribute, not to sell. Don't overtly push your Web site. Be subtle. If someone has asked for help or information, then reply, but make sure that you restrict your reply to the current discussion topic.

If your signature file includes your URL, with a one-sentence blurb or description of your business, that's all you need to do to promote your site. This is an effective way of drawing more traffic to your site.

Col Jones feels that participating in Internet discussions enhances your image online. However, he also feels that you should look at such participation as a long-term investment in the success of your online business.

Here's how to get started participating in newsgroups:

1. Query the DejaNews Usenet archives (www.dejanews.com), searching for keywords and topics which relate to your product or service. Make a list of the groups you find.
2. Subscribe to the groups, and monitor them. When a topic develops to which you can contribute, do so, using an effective signature line with your URL. Additionally, when a topic comes up where someone could benefit from your product, reply plugging your product—but make your reply short and to the point.
3. You will find that as you use newsgroups as a sales tool, you'll run out of time to monitor all the groups you're interested in. Check software archives for monitoring software. This type of software will notify you when a post is made to which you could reply. You will find that the same questions are asked repeatedly as new people subscribe to the groups, so this gives you ongoing opportunities to participate. You will also find people who will help you promote your product in the group, when you become known to them.

Consider an online newsletter

Online newsletters are popular. They allow readers to stay current in their areas of interest very simply—the information is delivered via e-mail directly to their mailbox. As an example of how quickly you can get subscribers for a newsletter, a travel company posted a sample of their newsletter to a Usenet group: they received 200 subscribers from the original posting. With each fresh posting to a different newsgroup, their subscriber list grew. The work involved was minimal, because the mailing list was handled automatically by an autoresponder program.

From a business point of view, a newsletter lets you get your name in front of readers as often as you want to send out issues. As well as advertising your own business via your newsletter, you can sell advertising space to other businesses once you have a respectable subscriber list. Additionally, with the number of Web sites growing, newsletters are one way to stand out from the crowd.

Jessica Torrance of Torrance Realty said she was dismayed by the number of other real estate agents in her city who had already gone online. She had to find some way to stand out from the crowd, and the way she chose was to create her own online newsletter. Why a newsletter?

> It creates awareness about my business, it reinforces my business identity, it distributes information, and it's a great way to advertise. When you consider that an online newsletter has no printing or mailing costs associated with it, it's an ideal way to get my message across. I'm by nature very chatty, so writing the thing was no problem—I've always got a lot to say.

The newsletter takes her around an hour a week to write, edit, and distribute. 'I consider that a good use of my time. I get at least a couple of inquiries each week because of the newsletter. And people print it out and take it home with them. I sold one house to a woman whose son printed out the newsletter and mailed it to her.'

What you put in your newsletter is up to you. Jessica's newsletter contains a couple of new property listings, some jokes, tips on selling your home, even recipes. 'Usually I have way too much material. I collect it during the week; I set aside anything that catches my eye.'

Jessica archives the newsletters on her Web site. 'It's useful content for the site. It means that people who are receiving the newsletter for the first time can go back and read previous issues if they want to.'

Jessica's newsletter tips

1. Gear your material towards what your readers are interested in. Not everyone will be interested in everything in each issue, but try to please as many people as possible.
2. What are people asking you? A newsletter is a good place to address concerns which a lot of your customers have.
3. Keep it short and simple to read. Most online newsletters are under 1000 words, including advertising.
4. Don't put the ads up-front—put your most useful information at the start of the newsletter. Think 'headline news' at the front of the newsletter.

Col Jones has another take on newsletters. No need to create your own newsletter, he says—advertise in someone else's. He even recommends advertising in e-mail newsletters over buying banner ads on other Web sites. He says it's more cost-effective. 'Readers like newsletters. They trust the person or organisation sending out the news-letter. That goodwill is passed on to companies who advertise in the newsletter. You gain instant credibility. It's as if the owner of the newsletter is vouching for you.'

Put your products' database online

If you have a catalogue of products, put the catalogue online. Consider the huge success of companies such as Amazon.com, which have done exactly that. The benefit to the consumer is that they can search for the item they want, and can order it immediately: no searching for a parking space or wasting time travelling. With an online catalogue, when you change the database the search results that visitors will get also change immediately. This means that you can remove items which have been sold (or perhaps add a 'sold' sticker to them), and can add new items. When you change the database, you're not dealing with HTML coding, so changes are easy to make. This flexibility is one of the main advantages of an online catalogue over the print version. However, many companies either fail to realise this, or fail to capitalise on it if they do. If you use an online catalogue, then keep it current; this may mean that you need to check it every day.

Although search engines can't index your database, you can add a daily or weekly specials page to your Web site—this page will be indexed on the search engines, and it also arouses curiosity and draws people to your site. Adding to your Web site is something you should keep in mind, whether you have an online database or not. Change your site frequently in response to comments from your visitors. You need commitment to make a Web site work. Nothing is sadder than to visit a site that hasn't changed in months. Col Jones says that when he visits a site like this: 'I usually decide against doing business with that company—if they don't care enough to keep the site updated, that lack of care will show in other ways as well. My reaction isn't unique. It's a common reaction, I've found.'

Give something away

As I have mentioned in earlier chapters, free is one of the most attention-getting words in the English language. Consider giving something away to get visitors to your site. This doesn't have to be a major item. It can be useful information, or an item that's computer-related, such as a screensaver. It shouldn't be something that you have to mail out, because the postage mounts up. Another option is to have a monthly competition, where you give away an item of some value. Use your imagination. If you sell big-ticket items, you could give away a holiday—the other end of the spectrum would be a bookmark. A T-shirt would be somewhere in the middle. To get more ideas on what others are giving away to draw people to their site, enter 'free' into one of the search engines.

Check out 'associates' programs (commissions)

Amazon.com was one of the first companies to promote this way of increasing sales. Basically, with an associates program, you put a link to another company on your Web site, and when a sale results from that link, you get a commission. With Amazon.com, you link to specific books in their database which fit in with your site's focus, in effect creating your own online bookstore. Amazon.com is said to pay up to 15 per cent commission on each sale.

Many other companies have associates programs, and you can certainly develop your own. As you form online relationships, offer your contacts a commission on referrals which result in a sale. This is a common way of doing business offline, and it works in the online environment as well.

Submit your site to search engines

With search engines proliferating on the Web, you may be tempted to either buy a program which submits your URL to search engines automatically, or to hire someone to make the submissions for you. However, it's more effective to do the submitting yourself. Each search engine has different preferences, works somewhat differently, has different requirements for keywords, and so on. No one knows as much about your business as you do. Hand-submitting means that you get the most from each search engine. When you've made the submissions, go to the search engine's site to make sure that your URL is displayed and that the link works as you expect it to.

Search engine submission requirements change constantly—it can seem that they change every day. Search engines are the most popular sites on the Web, and they're in heavy competition with each other. This means that they're always striving to attract more people to their site, thus the reason for the constant changes. This can be confusing for a small business person who's striving to keep their business up the top of the search engines' listings. Col Jones recommends that if your listing starts sliding in an engine, send an e-mail to learn why. It may be a factor that you can change quickly, and can thus regain your ranking, but you need to stay on top of it.

Pass on some of your savings to your customers

According to insurance company FAI, each online transaction only costs the company dollars, instead of tens of dollars, so they are passing on some of the savings to their Internet customers. On FAI's Web site, the online car insurance system offers speedy insurance quotes based on location, vehicle and driver history, simply by clicking on-screen boxes. If a customer decides to use FAI as the car's insurer, the complete transaction is handled online, and takes only five minutes.

The saving is in employees' time—insurance companies don't have to hire people to take details over the phone. The online customers enter their own details onto a secure Web page, and those details are posted directly into the companies' database, which then automatically creates a contract to be postal mailed to customers.

PROJECTING SALES FOR YOUR WEB SITE

You've done all the recommended tasks to promote your Web site. You've registered with the major search engines, directories and indexes, as well as sending press releases to traditional media, and advertising in newsletters and discussion groups. Your URL has a prominent place on your business card, and in your print advertising. You've paid for banner ads on carefully selected sites. How long will it take to start making real money from your Web site?

The consensus seems to be that it will take you around three to six months. However, there have been cases of sites generating brilliant sales in as little as 30 days. Although hits to your site are no indication of how many will convert to sales, as a rough guide you could count on 2 per cent to 10 per cent of hits eventually converting to sales.

Barbara Harris owns The Aussie Zoo in a Box, which sells quality Australian souvenirs. She recently took the business online.

Submit your site here! Useful URLs

The following are places to list your URL. Some give you the ability to list with several search engines from their location—you simply need to complete the form and follow the instructions:

http://addurl.com
http://altavista.digital.com/av/content/addurl.htm
http://autosubmit.com/promote.html
http://cashquest.com
http://whatuseek.com/addurl.htm
http://www.addme.com
http://www.adurl.com
http://www.boconline.com/t20pf.htm
http://www.broadcaster.co.uk
http://www.cashconnection.com/cashconnect
http://www.excite.com/info/add-url.html
http://www.findlink.com
http://www.funky-cat.com/SubmitForm.asp
http://www.hotbot.com/addurl.html
http://www.hypermart.net/consult/promo2.html
http://www.inetexchange.com/submit.htm
http://www.infomediacom.com/services/mastr125.htm
http://www.infoseek.com/AddUrl?pg=DCaddurl.html
http://www.linkexchange.com
http://www.lycos.com/addasite.html
http://www.mmgco.com/top100.html
http://www.netannounce.com/free16.html
http://www.netcreations.com/postmaster
http://www.submitnow.com
http://www.submit-it.com
http://www.submitshack.com
http://www.webcrawler.com/Help/GetListed/AddURLS.html
http://www.webpromote.com
http://www.worldprofit.com
http://www.yahoo.com/bin

Because we mention *kangaroos, koalas, wombats* in the meta tags we submit to search engines, we get a vast number of hits. Most of these are school children looking for information for projects. They won't be buying anything from us. However, we still manage to get around a 5 per cent conversion rate from hits to sales, which I'm pleased with.

Sales, rather than hits, are what count. Beware of making a large financial commitment to expanding your site, Barbara suggests, until you're sure that the site you have is generating a large number of *sales*. 'The formula for us,' she says, 'was: start slowly, test, modify, test some more, and build on what's working. We always knew that although the site was generating a few thousand hits a week, it's the number of hits which turn into sales which are important.'

While you're waiting for your site to begin generating sales, keep up your promotional activities. If your site is slow to generate traffic, don't worry. Your chief concern is always sales, not traffic. Your site may generate 2000 hits a day, but unless you can convert a respectable proportion to sales there's not much benefit.

ONLINE TALES OF WOE—BEWARE THE SCAM ARTISTS

A company which is making full use of the Internet for trading is New South Wales technology retailer, Harris Technology. The company's managing director, Ron Harris, told *Australian Personal Computer* magazine in late 1997 that over the past twelve months the company had done $1 million dollars worth of business online. He's very comfortable doing business online. He feels that there is no more exposure to fraud than with any ordinary credit card transaction made over the phone. Harris Technology uses a call-back system, to check delivery and other details, before a credit card order is processed.

However, the Internet has its share of scam artists. The following are some common scams that you should beware of.

Credit card cons

When you begin accepting credit card transactions, be sure to read the small print affecting online merchants. Ask your bank, or your card company, how they deal with fraud. If a customer supplies a stolen credit card number, and you ship the goods, are you out of pocket? The way card scams usually happen online is that a customer supplies a valid (but stolen) card number. The purchase is approved, and the goods are shipped—but not to the cardholder's address. Later, the transaction approval is denied, and the merchant is out of pocket.

How you handle the possibility of credit card fraud depends on the kind of transactions you're doing online. With medium to large sales, you will need a call-back process in place so that you can check that the person who supplied the card number owns the card. If you do a large number of small sales, you'll need to track the number of bogus transactions carefully. Again, be guided by the advice of your bank, or the credit card company.

Stealing copyright material from your site

Occasionally, entire Web sites are stolen. An unscrupulous person copies the site, and sells it to someone else, with their business name and details in place of the original site owner's. A variation of this ploy is to simply copy material from your site, and either use it on their own site without any credit to you, or use the material to spam newsgroups or mailing lists. Go to the sites listed below to learn how to deal with this.

Dealing with spam: stop forgery

Another online scam involves using someone else's identity. Usually this is just a nuisance. However, it can be serious if the person using your persona does something online, such as sending spam, which impacts negatively on your business. If someone is forging a spam as originating from you, go to this site to learn how to deal with it:

URL: http://www.bluemarble.net/~scotty/forgery.html

If you're receiving too much spam, go to this site:

URL: http://www.scambusters.org/stopspam

Spotting a scam

If you follow a few simple commonsense rules, you will never lose out to a scam artist. Here they are:

1. Anything that sounds too good to be true almost certainly is. If someone is offering you a targeted e-mail list at a giveaway price, check them out first. You should also beware of Web publishers with extensive inventories of advertising banners which they want to place on your site. Aim to be paid up-front, or get at least a 30-day guarantee on the payment. Although the companies are

legitimate, they are usually new companies, and if you give them too long a line of credit you may never see your money.

2. Whenever you deal with a company or an individual online, get all the contact details. Be wary of a company where you can't get a street address, and the phone and fax numbers of the principals. Check to see whether these contact details match the domain name registration. You should also check to see whether the phone and fax numbers work.

3. Know what you're agreeing to. The online world somehow seems more casual than the offline world. Maybe it's all the e-mail communication. However, no matter how casual and friendly it all seems, when you sign an agreement read it carefully. It's a legal document, so make sure that you understand what it means. If the language isn't clear, change it so that it means what you want it to mean. If you're in serious doubt, either don't sign, or have it vetted by a solicitor first.

4. Define all terms on an agreement. Eliminate any misunderstandings in your agreements by making sure that all terms (including jargon) are defined on the agreement itself. You may think you know what 'clickthrough' means; put the definition on the agreement itself, so everyone knows what it means, in plain English.

SALES TACTICS ON THE WEB

As a follow-up on scams, we'll discuss some dubious sales methods you may be tempted to use. Illegitimate sales tactics on the Internet include spam, which was covered in an earlier chapter. Don't be tempted to spam. There are many legitimate sales tactics on the Web, such as solicited e-mail advertising, and selling on newsgroups, which we cover below.

Legitimate e-mail advertising

Although I like receiving junk mail, both physical and virtual, others don't. Many Internet users are like me—they don't mind receiving e-mail in their areas of interest, as long as it's solicited e-mail, and as long as each message includes a few words on how to get off the mailing list if they want to do so.

So how do you go about creating an e-mailing list of people who want to hear from you? The simplest way is to create a *Please keep me informed* button on your Web page. You can notify the respondents when the site changes or when new products become available. You can also investigate the PostMaster Direct site, at URL: http://www.PostMasterDirect.com. This site encourages users to sign up for targeted e-mail. They claim three million e-mail addresses in over 3000 subject categories. You can obtain listings at around 30 cents per name. Initially, you browse through the database to select your target audience via keywords. You can refine your search in many ways. Once you have your list, you add your message and your mailing can go out immediately—everything is done for you, online. According to those who've used the service, it's cost-effective.

Selling on newsgroups

As mentioned in the last chapter, Usenet is a fantastic, up-to-the-minute resource. You can use it to garner intelligence on your competitors, as well as for research into products, prospects, investments and other areas—including making sales. However, unless you're posting your messages to those groups that are designed for advertising, you need to be subtle. As with e-mail, don't even consider spamming newsgroups.

Newsgroups are online communities. Each has its own code of conduct. If you transgress, expect to receive some caustic messages in your e-mail box.

Here are the basics for using Usenet:

1. Please stay on the topic. The people in alt.vegetarian won't be interested in an ad for your honey-cured bacon product.
2. Read any group for at least a week, to get a sense of the community attitudes, before posting.
3. Before you begin using a group to promote your business, contribute. Send topical information which members either enjoy, or can use in some way.
4. The FAQ file for the group will state the group's policy regarding advertising. Read it, and take it seriously. Pay attention to the instructions on how to post to the group.
5. Doubtless you'll want to send your messages about your product or service to more than one newsgroup. In this instance, make sure you cross-post, rather than re-post. There's a difference. When you cross-post, your message will only be seen once by someone

reading those groups to which you've posted. People who are interested in a topic, such as vegetarian food, will also read groups on related topics, such as low-fat cooking, and diets. They won't appreciate seeing ten or more copies of your re-posted message.

Newsgroups created for advertising

Your first impression of newsgroups such as alt.biz, which consist solely of ads, might be cynical. Who reads these groups? While it's doubtful that these advertising newsgroups are read in their entirety by many people, remember that these advertisements will come up in some of the search engines. If someone is thinking of buying a product or service and is looking for information or for the best price, they will use one of the search engines, or Deja News (URL: http://www.dejanews.com), the search engine created specifically to search Usenet. Assuming that the keyword they've entered is in your newsgroup posting, Deja News, as well as Excite and Yahoo, will all find it. This means that you can effectively use the ads-only newsgroups if you want to. And the biggest benefit of these ads-only groups is, of course, that they're free—you can reach millions of people just by typing in your message and sending it to the groups you choose.

In conclusion, making sales on the Internet is not so different from making sales offline. Use commonsense techniques, as Ray Toms of Moonshine Supplies does, and you will do well. Remember it's vital that you target a niche market. Of all the millions of Internet users, most won't be interested in what you're selling. The more narrowly you can define your niche (within reason) the more you'll be able to make those people aware of your products. For example, I'm a member of several writers' mailing lists. On those lists, the same people's names continually pop up as contributors. They're not blatantly selling their products: they're asking a question, or answering a question put by another member of the group. Nevertheless, their URL and the product they sell always appear in their signature lines, and from writing to them off-list, I know that they attract lots of new customers with their contributions to mailing lists and newsgroups. Slowly and steadily they're building name recognition among their niche market, and they're making money.

This chapter has given you lots of ways to be proactive as you sell in cyberspace—so, just do it!

The commonsense approach to selling online—Ray Toms and Moonshine Supplies

Ray Toms sells home-brewing equipment and supplies at Moonshine Supplies in New Zealand. He took his business online in 1995, and he has a refreshingly commonsense view of what it takes to make sales online. He believes that you don't need a fancy Web page for online success, nor do you need to worry too much about online transactions—he doesn't have a credit card facility, for example. What you do need to do is be responsive, and provide good service.

He says:

When we set up our Web page I was completely ignorant about the Internet, so I had a professional design my page—but I've been updating it myself since then. I believe that one of the keys to our success is that we have a simple page with few graphics. I get almost daily compliments on it. It doesn't have bells and whistles, but it does have a lot of hard information that's difficult to find elsewhere. I don't go in for frames, banners and navigation bars. I am basically a retailer with a physical shop; the Internet is just an extension of that retail business.

He gives three main reasons for his success:

I operate in a niche market and provide information which is not easily available from other sources. I provide a real person for people to deal with—I have a personal home page linked to my business page telling people about myself, providing a photo as well as a real address and telephone number. I have a policy of turning around my e-mail within 24 hours—I'm amazed at the number of responses I get where people say that they are grateful for a prompt reply. The implication is that many people are not responding to e-mail quickly.

He believes that doing business on the Internet is basically no different from doing business in his physical store. 'In my retail store I have three guiding principles to give me my marketing edge—excellent service, expert knowledge and the best products. The Internet is no different. If I can't provide those three things on the Internet as well, I have no right trading there.'

As for online transactions, he freely admits that he doesn't make it easy for people to do business with him:

I don't provide a secure facility for online transactions at the moment. Only one bank currently offers that facility in New Zealand, and I don't want to change banks. Nor do I want to go offshore. So it's true, I don't make it easy for people to order from me. I also don't have an online order form, for example. This means that I don't get impulse buys, but it also means that people who want to buy need to start up an e-mail dialogue with me. This has meant that my credit card fraud has been nil.

Boosting your Internet sales

1. You build sales by building traffic to your site. Meta tags—the key-words—that you submit to the major search engines are important. Col Jones advises you to take out a thesaurus, and go through every possible permutation of descriptions for your site. You should also use all the possible spelling permutations. 'Even misspellings. Use both American and English spellings.'

2. Advertise and network. 'Think about what you do to promote the offline part of your business, and work out ways of doing it online', Col recommends. 'Remember that the rules of business promotion don't change just because your business is online.'

3. Close sales. Closing sales on the Internet may be more difficult than it is in the offline world. Col says this is particularly true for people who operate service businesses online:

   People like to see you and talk to you when they buy a service. This isn't possible online, and you need to think of ways of getting around that. How do you help people to feel that they know you? One of the best ways is to show who you are: that is, have a page on your Web site which includes your photograph, and tells something about you and your business. Be prepared to engage in dialogue with people via e-mail, sure, but also don't hesitate to pick up the phone.

4. Offer guarantees to your customers, so that they will feel more comfortable dealing with you.

Making contacts

Contacts are vital when you take your business online. In this chapter, we'll discuss the management of your contact information, and how to go about finding new contacts. Then we'll discuss turning your contacts into sales—and since this will involve more writing than you're probably used to, we'll cover the basics of effective online communications, including building contacts through online discussion groups. In addition, we'll look at the various kinds of database marketing lists which are available on the Internet.

NETWORKING ONLINE

The Internet is a computer network, but it's also a vast business network. It offers opportunities that you may never have considered before. You need to take the time to tap into this global network. Using your networking skills will expand your online business. You *are* working on your networking skills, aren't you? If the term 'networking' puts you off, think of it as making friends. We'd all rather do business with someone we know, and networking is basically getting to know as many other people as possible.

Sally Seary runs a marketing business, and has always been keenly aware of the importance of networking. She says: 'Networking is the basis of any business. Networking with others makes all your business activities more effective.' She believes in using the Internet to develop new contacts. 'You can establish business relationships online more easily than you can offline, because it's easier to learn more about people before you try to contact them for the first time.' She recommends running a Web search and a Usenet search on companies you're unfamiliar with. 'The more you know about them, the more power you have.'

Making contacts online is easy, but managing the acquired information about your contacts, so that it is useful to you, requires some thought and resourcefulness.

Jenny Firestone runs Firestone & Wallace PR, a public relations company which she recently took online. Easier networking, she says, was her main reason for taking her business online:

> I specialise in non-fiction author promotions, as well as in health and fitness, and small business promotions. Most of my media contacts are online now, and they prefer e-mail news releases because they're easier to manage than letters or faxes. I found I needed a Web site to let reporters have easy access to our releases. Having my own Web site means that I can provide a better service—if a reporter is writing a story at midnight, they can access the site and locate the information they need.

The problem for Jenny was managing the flood of new contacts she was making online—she found she needed contact management software. She says that for years the business cards she collected were her contact database:

> It worked. Whenever I received a card I wrote three things on the back: the date I met the person, where I met them, and any follow-up I had to do. However, when I went online and started getting around twenty e-mail messages a day from new contacts, I had to find a new way. The way I handled it was to save and print out the messages. Finally, I broke down and bought contact management software. It was a hassle learning it, but now it's great.

While everyone I spoke to appreciated the ease of online communications, many also found it difficult to set up a new computer-based and online-focused information management system which worked for them. Most use either a database application, or a contact management program. The best choice for you will probably be a program that you already know how to use. Barry Michaels of Boots Online swears by Info Select, a personal information manager. However, you can also use a spreadsheet or a database application to store contacts. Ideally, you should give some thought to how you will use contact information, in order to help you make a choice of the many options available. If you choose to use a database application, it may be worthwhile having a computer consultant set it up for you so that it does everything you need it to, such as perform mail mergers, create invoices and statements, and print out customised reports.

Contact management checklist

Here are some questions to ask yourself about your contact management needs:

- How much information do you need to store on each contact? If you only need basic information, such as names and addresses, phone numbers and e-mail addresses, any spreadsheet program can store them adequately. If you need to store detailed customer account information, such as items purchased and amounts owing, you will need a relational database application, such as Microsoft Access.
- Do you need access to contact information when you're away from your desktop computer? If this is a primary requirement, you can look at Personal Information Managers, such as Lotus Organizer, or Franklin Quest Ascend. These kinds of programs will print to a variety of paper-based organisers. They also interface with small hand-held PCs, such as the Palm Pilot, which are popular with people who spend a lot of time on the road.
- Do you think that keeping up with the Internet part of your business will take a couple of hours each day? If you'll be spending a lot of time interacting by e-mail, store your contact information in the Address Books which come with your browser.

Finding new contacts step by step

With upwards of 40 million people accessible online, it's easy to find people who may be interested in your product or service. When you've found them, you make your offerings to them. However, you also need to build ongoing relationships with people who will refer clients to you, or who will tell other people about your product.

But how do you start? Where do you begin to look for these people? Ask yourself some questions:

1. In what fields are the people who might refer clients to you? The people who could refer clients to you might be in banking, in investment, or in the building trades, etc. Make a list of these fields.

2. In what fields would you like to expand your client base? If most of your clients are doctors, perhaps you want more doctors' names, or perhaps you want dentists and lawyers. Make a list, again.

3. In what fields don't you have clients, but would welcome some? For example, if you're an investment consultant, you may have many clients who are lawyers. You might decide that doctors would also make good prospects, so you also want to add doctors to your client list. Make another list. By now you should have a list of several business fields in which you're interested.

4. Now you need to know where your prospects 'hang out' online. Many of your prospects will participate in e-mail discussion groups, which are usually known just as 'mailing lists'. The next step is to find the online mailing lists covering the fields you've listed. Go to URL: http://www.liszt.com (the Liszt Searchable Directory of E-mail Mailing Lists and Newsgroups). Enter the fields you've listed (one at a time) into the query box. In addition, if you already have clients who are online, ask them what mailing lists they participate in.

5. Join the mailing lists you've identified. I don't recommend that you spam any of the lists you join—in other words, don't blatantly use the groups to promote yourself and your business. Either start a discussion where it would be appropriate for you to mention your product or service, or just join in the discussions, and allow your sig file to do the work for you. Sig files are great advertising. Always include your e-mail address and your URL in any sig file; your e-mail address is vital, because some e-mail clients strip out the addresses of senders.

6. Read the sig files of the people who send messages to your target lists. Send a *personalised* message to those who are in your target groups. By personalised, I mean an e-mail message which is similar to a personal letter. Tell each person where you saw their name (on which mailing list or newsgroup), and introduce yourself and

your business. Your letter should not be an advertising pitch. Ask a question, or share some information which they may find useful.

7. You can also place a line at the end of your own sig file: 'I am looking for solicitors, doctors, building contractors (*insert your own preferred fields here*) for possible business referrals.'

8. Finally, if you have the time, you can start your own e-mail discussion group.

By the time you've completed all of the above—and it does take time—your online contacts will have grown by leaps and bounds.

Sales contacts aside, some of the best contacts you'll make online are those people who are either in the same industry, or who are also doing what you're doing—taking their business online and working to make that business successful. Alexa Parisi of Gemstone Dreaming said that her most useful contacts have come from a jewellery-making e-mail list she is on, as well as from a jewellery newsgroup. She says that she has had nothing but kindness whenever she has posted a question to either group:

> The first time I posted a question I was nervous. I'd heard that Usenet groups could be rough on newcomers. My first posting to the newsgroup received two public responses, as well as six private responses. Two of the people who responded have become valued members of my personal network. I know that I can call on them any time I strike a problem with something I'm doing. I've also found a US distributor for my stones through the newsgroup.

Budget time for managing your online contacts

Building your network of contacts is building your business. However, many business owners do it in a haphazard fashion. They'd like to devote more time to making contacts, but they don't have the time. Time management is a problem for everyone—no one has enough time. When you take your business online, time management will become even more of an issue, if it's an issue for you already. Marianne Kaser is a business consultant who runs time-management seminars. She believes that one mistake many small business owners make is taking on too much:

> Invariably, when they become used to the speed with which they can make things happen online, they try to cram in even more tasks. I had

Online discussions: one way to draw traffic to your site.

one client who was selling lambskin car-seat covers. He was doing very well. Within a few months of going online, he was selling covers to New Zealand, South Africa and the UK. The problem was he hadn't counted on so much expansion so quickly. He had all kinds of difficulties and wanted to know how he could manage his time more effectively. I told him the best thing he could do was to take care of his health. I had him take a week off and rethink his business processes. The time away gave him perspective, and he took on a partner.

Marianne's primary time-management advice is to budget your time:

Building a network of contacts is building your future business income. I recommend that every business owner devote 30 minutes a day to contacts. This sounds like a lot of time, especially to those people who are working alone in their business. If you don't have that time, then perhaps you should think of ways in which you could make time. Can you subcontract the work which someone else could do, such as the bookkeeping?

Making online contacts is cost-effective

Making new contacts and using them to build your online business takes time—or money. However, it has one enormous benefit: it's cheap. At a recent Chamber of Commerce and Industry meeting, I spoke with a local businessperson who'd just taken his business online. He wanted to know how he could build his network of contacts. I recommended that he join newsgroups and online mailing lists, and contribute to the discussions. This process works. Each contribution you make to a newsgroup or e-mail discussion list is archived, and will thus be available for years to come. It promotes your business inexpensively, and it's also enjoyable. However, his attitude was that he didn't have the time to spare to do all this. I told him that he had to find the time. The alternative was to spend money buying advertising in banner ads, or perhaps sponsoring an informational site. He had to find a way to drive traffic to his site.

TURNING ONLINE CONTACTS INTO SALES

Now that you've made online contacts, let's see how you go about turning them into sales.

You will find that your online sales technique requires different skills from your in-person sales technique. This is because most of the contacts you make online will be made through writing. You need to:

- become comfortable using your writing skills to build your contacts;
- be proactive;
- follow up; and
- realise that you won't make a sale with the first e-mail exchange.

Let's discuss these factors in detail.

Build your contacts and business: say it in writing

Alexa Parisi says that although she was uncomfortable with the amount of correspondence it took to make sales online at first, she quickly got used to it. It was a process of building trust, she says:

When people come into my shop, they can pick up a stone, handle it, see it in different lights, and watch the play of colours across the stone. But if people see a stone that they're interested in on the Web site, they need more information. They need me to tell them more about the stone, to describe it more fully. Collectors often want a couple of photographs of a stone before they make a decision. Basically, they want to be convinced that someone they meet online is a real person, with a real business; it takes time to build comfort and trust.

She also believes that, although an online sale may take a week or longer to make, the actual time she spends in making the sale is shorter:

When a customer comes into the shop, I'll spend upwards of an hour showing stones and discussing them, then making the sale. My online customers tend to be more knowledgeable. They've done their research, they know what they want. They also know the prices of comparable stones. I may exchange four or five e-mail messages to make an initial sale, but the total time is around half an hour or less. Any subsequent sales I make to this client will take even less time, because they now know me and know my business.

She also says she does more repeat business through the Web site than through her shop:

Part of all the writing to and fro is that you build up a relationship with people. Once they buy a stone and they're happy with it, they'll get in touch with me and buy again because they have formed that relationship. My online customers are my biggest customers. I take huge orders now—for example, offline my biggest sale was around $3000 for a packet of stones. Online, I routinely take orders for $50 000.

You may need help to build your writing skills. Edie of Edie's Herbals took a business communications course before she took her business online. 'I was resting up from an operation, and I did a business-writing correspondence course. It was the best decision I ever made. It gave me the confidence to know that I could express myself clearly in writing.'

She suggests that before you start writing an e-mail message, you make a list of the things you want to say. 'It's not an outline. I hated outlines at school; I think most people do. And if you outline in a point-by-point fashion, it comes across as stilted. You want to write the same way you speak. It should be conversational, so the person you're writing to gets a sense of who you are as a person.'

Another tip is to read your e-mail messages aloud before you send them:

> E-mail is conversational. You can always tell if someone is new to e-mail, because their messages are very stiff and formal. In the beginning, I read all my messages aloud, especially the ones I was sending to a mailing list, so that I could get the tone right. It takes practice to sound as though you're speaking rather than writing. Reading a message aloud also makes you aware of any unintended meaning your message might have. You need to be very aware of the tone of your message.

Jenny Firestone's tip is to check your e-mail messages for spelling, grammar and punctuation mistakes before you send them out:

> I think it's courteous to do that. I'm more aware of it because I'm in communications, of course, but I think taking care with the basics applies to any business. If people think you don't care about how your messages look, they'll have doubts about whether you care about the rest of your business. You wouldn't go to a meeting with tomato sauce or mayonnaise stains on your tie, would you?

You should also try to keep your e-mail messages reasonably short. Alexa Parisi says she receives a lot of e-mail because she's on several e-mail lists, and that she often deletes messages where the sender won't come to the point in the first paragraph:

> Put the main point of your message in the first paragraph, or even in the first sentence. Make sure that your entire message fits on the screen, so that the person reading it doesn't have to scroll. If you're replying to a message, put your reply at the top of the message, rather than at the bottom.

Be proactive

If you hate cold calling, the Internet can take some of the angst out of the process for you—but it won't relieve you of all of it. Jenny says that she is a shy person, who hates cold calling:

> E-mail makes it easier to make an initial contact. However, you still have to make that first contact. I'm always looking for new business, and I send out a couple of introductory e-mail messages every day. There's always a point to my messages—they aren't simply spam—so

each message takes quite a bit of research and thought. For example, I'll research the business that the person is in, and I'll visit their Web site if they have one, so that I know as much as I can about them.

She believes that she gets a better response to her introductory e-mail messages than she does to the postal letters she sends out:

Part of the reason is that e-mail is more casual. People don't seem to feel that they're under an obligation to give you business if they respond to an e-mail message. And part of it, I'm sure, is that e-mail can be friendlier—you can mention something you saw on their Web site which was well done. Another thing I often do is enclose an article about their company I've found on the Web, or a Usenet message about them that they might not have seen.

Following up

Again and again, those people who have had the most success with their Web sites emphasised the importance of following up on your e-mail messages. Jenny Firestone receives around 200 e-mail messages a day:

Depending on what else is happening, I might not get around to replying to the messages until late that night, but I always reply on the same day I receive them. Although I'm not perfect! Occasionally I can't get the information that someone wants immediately, so I'll put their message into my Follow Up folder. Then a week or two later, I'll come across the message, and realise that I haven't got back to the person. I feel it's always best to admit the error, and let them know what happened. It only takes a moment, and people remember that you *did* respond.

Jenny also makes good use of the Send This Page To button in her browser:

It's important that you stay in touch with people, especially past clients—or your new prospects. They may not have any work for you at the moment, but if you don't stay in touch, they will have forgotten you by the time they do have some. So whenever I see an interesting piece on the Web, I'll send it out to clients.

Communications is Jenny's field, so here are several more of her tips for following up with contacts:

- Automate as much of your contact management processes as you can. Have a plan of action for current clients, prospects, and past clients. This plan should ensure that you make contact with all your clients at least once in each three-month period. Jenny says that when she adds a prospect to her database, she schedules tasks for the prospect—send information, send follow-up, make phone contact, and so on.

- Prepare information packs which you send out to new contacts, and always have a supply of these packs on hand.
- Check your e-mail at least twice a day, and try to respond within 24 hours if you can.

As in the 'real' world, it often takes a few exchanges to turn a contact into a client. Be prepared for several e-mail exchanges to allow your prospect to become comfortable with the idea of doing business with you. Jenny suggests that you be creative. 'Always think about the other person. What can you do for them? I've always found that you'll get, as long as you're prepared to give first.'

MAKING CONTACTS THROUGH MAILING LISTS AND NEWSLETTERS

Many of the people running information sites said that the easiest way to make and build contacts was to create a sense of community on your site. Jon Bard of the Children's Book Insider, a virtual bookshop, says that what has helped his site most is the work he's done to make his site a resource for potential customers, not just an ad billboard. He says: 'Adding message boards, chatrooms, industry links and so on to your site are cheap and easy to do, but they're a wonderful thing to do for your visitors. They'll come back to your site, and they'll tell their friends about the site as well.'

Jon started out garnering contact information from his visitors using a simple guest book program. This gave him enough e-mail addresses to mail out a free newsletter each month. He says that the newsletter may become his new profit centre for the site:

We send it out as a free monthly mailing to everyone who signs our guest book or requests our catalogue from our autoresponder. It's half useful info and half promo stuff about us. It's an excellent way to remind visitors about us, and to put our marketing message in front of potential customers again and again. The next step is to start selling ad space in the newsletter, as it's now up to 8000 readers. Primarily, however, the newsletter is a great opportunity for more promotion, as we post notices about how to get a free subscription to it on message boards on other sites, in newsgroups, in various Internet announcement lists, and so on.

Jon recommends a guest book program for every site. 'It's a way to gather contact information painlessly. It's also targeted contact information. These are people who visited your site, and want to let you know that they're interested in what you do, even if they didn't buy anything.'

Building a marketing list from Usenet discussion groups

Many of the people whose Web sites attract attention spend hours each week on Usenet, joining discussions and promoting their business with their contributions by using signature files with their URLs. This can be a lengthy process, if you try to do it all manually.

Marianne Kaser recommends a service called Intellinews, located at URL: http://www.intellinews.com. Intellinews is a smart agent, a software program which searches Usenet newsgroups for postings which match a subscriber's filtering criteria. For example, Marianne says that her filters include the terms: 'time management' and 'productivity'. When a match is found, the subscriber receives a notice via e-mail. Marianne says:

> When I receive the message, I read it and fire off a message to the group telling them about my Web site. I also provide other information which I have ready to e-mail, depending on what the poster's need happens to be. I'm not spamming the group—I'm answering a need. Using Intellinews means that I spend less time monitoring discussions.

She believes that the program is worth the $US12 annual subscription fee. 'Whenever I post to Usenet, I get an increase in traffic.'

Creating your own mailing list

One of the easiest ways to build your contacts database is to create an online newsletter or an online discussion e-mail group. It's a way to stay in touch with customers who may be interested in your product or service, but who may not be ready to buy just yet. You create the newsletter, then send it out via a mailing list program to people who have chosen to receive it. Collect the names of subscribers by placing a button on your Web site: *Please enter your e-mail address if you would like to receive our monthly (daily/weekly) newsletter*. Or, if you want to

Database marketing on the Internet

What about database marketing on the Internet? Can you buy an effective targeted list online? Although there are many sites which sell mailing lists made up of e-mail addresses, the best list you use will be one that you've created yourself. Everyone I spoke to who had taken their business online successfully emphasised the point of creating your own mailing list, as Jon Bard of the Children's Book Insider did. He now has a useful list of 8000 names. Each of these people know who he is, what his business does, and they trust him.

Marianne Kaser says that the problem with database marketing lists which you buy is that the messages you send to these people will be perceived as spam. 'They don't know you. They haven't asked to receive a mailing from you. Building up your own mailing lists may take time, but so does building a successful business. Whether or not to buy a mailing list is a personal choice, but I recommend creating your own list.'

form a discussion group: *Please enter your e-mail address if you want to join our discussion group*.

Programs which service mailing lists don't require any programming experience. Several sites on the Web will create and host e-mail discussion groups for you, and will also send out your newsletters. You simply forward each edition of the newsletter to the Web site when it's ready. If you want to set up a discussion group, all messages from members will be sent to the site's servers, and will then be forwarded to everyone in the group. Some sites charge according to the amount of traffic on the list; that is, by the megabyte. Other sites will host a list for you even if you have a budget of zero—advertising covers the list's costs.

You can create a free discussion group at Coollist (URL: http://www.coollist.com). This service is completely free, but a small advertising message appears on the bottom of each e-mail. You can get an e-mail discussion operating within minutes. Coollist even provides a programming code to place on your Web site so that visitors can subscribe to your list by filling in their e-mail address.

Making contacts online is easy. Managing those contacts—and finding the time to do it—is less easy. However, it's vital to the success of your online business.

chapter 8

Public relations

In this chapter, we'll discuss public relations. In a sense, public relations is similar to the networking we discussed in the previous chapter. However, rather than building your relationships with individual contacts, you'll be building your relations with your various 'publics'. These publics can include your customers, your suppliers, the government—anyone who interacts with, or has any influence on, your business. This chapter includes information on generating publicity for your Web site and using Web communications, as well as tips for keeping your business name and activities circulating.

Public relations isn't well understood among Australian small business people. Usually, if they think of public relations at all, it's thought of in terms of a news release or as advertising. The *Macquarie Dictionary* defines public relations as: *the practice of promoting goodwill among the public for a company, government body, individual or the like; the practice of working to present a favourable image.* Small business people tend to think of public relations as something which applies only to large companies. But even if you've never thought of public relations and the image you and your business present, you should think of them both when you launch your business online. Why? Because it's simple for anyone who wants to know more about you to enter your name and your business's name into a search engine. Not only will your Web site come up, but any postings which have been made about you, your business or your products or services in newsgroups or in mailing lists will also come up. With just a few minutes of digging, it's easy for anyone who's interested in you to learn just what kind of image you have online. Like it or not, you can't hide online.

The easiest way to think of public relations is as effective communications, and communications are a part of every stage of both your online and offline marketing strategies. It's not merely the occasional press release that you fire off to the media. It's building your company's profile, and is a part of everything you do, from the labels on your products to your logo and your invoices. Because your presence on the Web is highly visible, you can use this high visibility both to inform visitors to your site about your products and services, and to gain information from those visitors which would be difficult, or impossible, to gain in any other way.

Public relations on the Web differs from the public relations you do offline, in that your communications can be much more immediate. Additionally, they can be much more focused because you can segment your markets. Rather than thinking of your customers as a group, the online environment allows you to build individual relationships with each of your customers. It's worth spending some time analysing how and why you communicate on the Web, and how you can improve your communications feedback with your various publics—customers, prospects, staff, competitors, and suppliers. If you're aware of the importance of communications and public relations online, you can work to create goodwill for yourself and your business. And while this may not seem to have an immediate effect, you will eventually see the benefit to your business.

In 1995 Kirsten Woodward

Be image-conscious

- You can't hide online. Not only are your communications archived, but so is every comment about you and your business.
- You should think about the image you're creating with every communication that you send online; be aware that every public communication you create online, whether it's your Web site, or a posting in a newsgroup or mailing list, has an effect on your company's image. That image can last a long time, and if it's a negative one, it can be tough to change. Strive to make your image a positive one.
- Although your business will take time to build in the online world, once you've established a presence it will become easier; other businesses will link to your Web site, and they'll refer people to you.

opened a small restaurant on Sydney's North Shore. Unfortunately, the restaurant closed six months after it opened. Although in 1995 most Australians' contact with the online world was via CompuServe, Kirsten nevertheless created a home page for her restaurant and began promoting it online. She laughs as she says:

> When the restaurant closed I took down the Web site, but the thing won't die. Four years later, I still get around five e-mails a month about the restaurant, asking for more recipes—I put some of our recipes online—and directions to the restaurant. I'm tempted to open another restaurant to capitalise on the fame of the first one.

GENERATING PUBLICITY FOR YOUR WEB SITE

You can get the word out about your new site in various forums around the World Wide Web. The following are the major areas which you should consider:

- announcing your site on Usenet;
- getting a 'cool sites' listing; and
- getting listed in meta-sites.

Let's look at these areas in more detail.

Announcing your site on Usenet

When you publicly launch your site by announcing it on Usenet, it means that your announcement will come up in the DejaNews search engine and in any other search engines which index Usenet postings. It's the easy way for people to find you, whether they look for you this week or in three years' time. Therefore, making such an announcement is well worth doing. Here's how to do it. Create a new message in your newsreader announcing your site. Be sure to include the URL—you'd be surprised how many people send wonderful announcements about their new Web site, but manage to leave out the most important information.

Send the announcement to the following newsgroups:

comp.internet.net–happenings
comp.infosys.www.announce
misc.news.inet.announce

> ### Creating a message in your newsreader
>
> Writing a message in your newsreader is much the same as writing an e-mail message. Newsreaders are part of all major Web browsers: Netscape Navigator, Microsoft Internet Explorer, and Opera. To create a new message, open your newsreader, and choose New News Message from the File menu. Type the name of the newsgroup in the To: box, and your subject in the Subject: box. Type your message in the Message area, and hit the Send button. When next you connect to the Internet, your newsgroup message will be sent.

These three forums are the main Internet announcement areas. You should also search through the Usenet database of newsgroups to discover which other groups would be interested in news of your site.

Do people take any notice of these announcements? I do, and I know that many other media people do too. I scan around ten Usenet groups at least a couple of times a week looking for new sites. Once a month, I search DejaNews, again looking for new sites in my areas of interest. I'm also a member of several mailing lists which focus on new Web sites.

Many of the people I spoke to for this book weren't aware that they could use the Usenet announcement groups as a way of launching their site. Those who were aware, and who did announce their site, received feedback and inquiries—often many months, or in a couple of cases several *years*, after the initial announcement. You should also remember that it's never too late to use the announcement newsgroups, so if you haven't announced your Web site to the online world yet, get right on it. It's a fast, simple and efficient way to promote your site—and it's free.

Obtaining a 'cool' site listing

All of the major search engines feature 'cool' sites and give them free publicity. You can nominate your site for a cool-site listing; if you're successful, it will definitely drive a lot of new traffic to your site. It's worth nominating your site if your site is unique, or if it includes a lot of hard-to-find material. Brian Fallon, who has a free small business training course on his site, has had his site mentioned several times in cool-site listings. He says he deliberately set out to gain cool-site attention:

There are a lot of training courses online, and I wanted to make my site stand out. I knew that one way I could do this would be by making the site an information resource, and then by nominating it as a cool site. I'm pleased with the cool-site listings I've received; they increased traffic tenfold in the weeks they appeared.

Basically, think of a cool-site listing as a site review. There are hundreds of sites online which give listings of reviewed 'cool' sites. Find them by entering 'cool site' into a search engine.

Getting listed in the meta-sites

Several meta-sites have been developed on the Web. They're a further development of the hierarchical subject guides. They help people using the Web to find relevant sites without hours of searching. Meta-sites are divided into special interest topics. Reviewers, called 'guides' on sites like The Mining Company (URL: http://www.miningco.com), provide weekly articles on their chosen topics, and review Web sites which are related to their topic in those articles. Suite 101 is another well-known meta-site (URL: http://www.suite101.com). Reviewers for meta-sites are always looking for new and interesting sites. To gain a site review, contact the person who writes the articles in your subject area at each individual meta-site, and tell them about your site. Once your site has been reviewed by a meta-site, it will retain its listing, thus providing ongoing publicity for your site.

USING WEB COMMUNICATIONS FOR BETTER PUBLIC RELATIONS

Your Web PR efforts fall into these main areas: product or service development, marketing, sales, after-sales service, and altruism. Remember that each of these communications is a chance to improve your image on the Web: it's a public relations exercise.

Product or service development

This is a form of market research, but you should be aware that it's also public relations. The Web gives you the opportunity to try out new ideas quickly and cheaply. As you interact with people who access your site, and with people on Usenet and on mailing lists, you have an immense opportunity to find out what products people want that you can supply. If you come up with a new product or service, you can offer it on your Web site to see what the reaction to it is. Each interaction, of course, is a public relations exercise for your business.

For example, Brian Fallon set up a Web site for his accountancy business. Originally, the site was simply a way to find new clients. However, the site quickly became a way for Brian to cut down on his travelling time—his clients could send him their monthly accounts via FTP (File Transfer Protocol). Then Brian saw an opportunity for another way to use the site. He had always known that there was a need for a small business management course for people who had never run a business before. He wanted to create such a course, put it on a CD-ROM, and sell the CD-ROM on the site. He decided that his Web site provided a way for him to get feedback on the course while he was developing it, so that he could modify it to make it as useful as possible.

While he was trialling the information for the course on his Web site, access to it was free. The course was popular, and he started receiving so many requests for advice that he started a new business as a small business consultant. 'The online course I developed remains free,' Brian says. 'Although it was never intended that way, it was and is a great public relations exercise for my new management training business, as well as for my accountancy business.'

Marketing

E-mail lets you get the word out about what's happening in your business as never before. You can send information to prospects, current customers, consultants, and media people. Remember that each communication is a form of public relations. It should enhance the image of your company.

Sales

Public relations is definitely a part of selling. You need to be prompt in answering inquiries about your products. Getting the product to your clients as fast as possible is also good public relations.

After-sales service

Good after-sales service is brilliant public relations. Each sale you make can be a springboard to future sales, if your customer is pleased with the product and tells others about it. Stevie Gordon sells sporting equipment through a Web site. She makes a point of calling each of her clients within two days of a piece of equipment being delivered:

> I want to make sure they're happy. I try to get them on the phone if I can; if not, I'll send a fax or I'll e-mail them. Do they have any questions? Are they finding the product easy to use? I'll chat to them about how others are using that particular piece of equipment. It's also an opportunity for me to ask them for a referral. Do they know of anyone else who might be interested in my products?

Altruism

Doing something without expecting a reward pays its own reward in good public relations. Jenny Rayburn is a public relations consultant, and she says that the way the business owner sees their business is vital. They need to feel that they are part of the community. In the case of the Internet, it's a global community. 'Sure, it's great to concentrate on the bottom line. But it's also good to develop some altruism. I can't prove it, but I feel that companies that try to help people as well as sell them something do better in the long term. Besides, helping people makes you feel good and, if you feel good about what you're doing, that surely is worthwhile.'

Jenny suggests that you think about how your site can provide a useful service, such as a database of articles, free advice, and so on—something that the visitor can access immediately for free, and that will also make the visitor want to return to the site.

KEEPING YOUR BUSINESS NAME CIRCULATING

The Web is increasingly a resource for journalists. The OzEmail Press Release Centre (URL: http://www.pressrelease.com.au) has been set up to take advantage of this fact. Journalists sign up for free to receive news releases in categories which interest them. Businesses sign on and pay a monthly fee, with no restrictions on the number of releases sent out, and the site sends the media releases around the world via e-mail. To use the service, you submit your release via a Web-based form, choosing the date and the time of the announcement, as well as the appropriate categories.

Jenny says that the main thing to remember about a news release is that it should contain some news. It doesn't have to be earth-shattering, however:

> If you're adding a unique product line, and you're excited about it, that's news. If you've been written up in other media, that's also news. Other items you could feature would be special promotions, such as competitions you're running, opening a store at a new location, and so on.

The Internet gives you a whole new arena in which to promote your business. However, as you use online resources, keep your public relations image in mind—your business is highly visible on the Web. Make sure that the image you create is the one you want for your business.

Company contacts and suppliers

Your business relationships with other companies and with your suppliers are vital. The Internet can help you to enhance the relationships you already have with other companies, through clearer and faster communications, and it can also help you to form new relationships. In this chapter, we'll help you to start forming working relationships with other companies.

As of late 1998, business-to-business commerce forms the backbone of the Web. Your Internet connection gives you wide access to other companies, both in Australia and all over the world. You may be looking for distributors or distributorships, for other companies with which to form strategic alliances, for tenders, for suppliers—in fact, for almost anything. The Internet is the ideal hunting ground to find the companies that fill your requirements, because all you need to do is to enter your requirements into a search engine and a list of companies which match them will come up.

Col Jones encourages the companies he deals with to actively pursue alliances with others, both in Australia and overseas. He says:

> The Internet allows small businesses to cooperate with each other, to pool their resources, and to develop their ideas. It's simple for them to find and contact each other. For example, I created a Web site for a dairy farmer on the south coast of New South Wales. He's the head of a cooperative of dairy farmers setting up a cheese-making factory. He started exchanging e-mail messages about cheese-making with a farmer

in the US. Through this farmer, he located a US company which was producing a new low-fat cheese which is very successful on the US market. They did some market research, and the NSW cooperative discovered that the low-fat cheese should do well here also. The cooperative has just signed to make the low-fat cheese in Australia, under licence—before their factory is even finished.

The simplest way to start networking for new business relationships is to join one of the many business-to-business development networks on the Internet. ProfNet, which is run by Nancy Roebke, is a professional networking group with over 30 chapters throughout the US and worldwide. ProfNet is a great site which gives you a swag of information on developing company contacts. You can also join ProfNet, either by forming a local chapter of the organisation in your area or by joining an online ProfNet chapter. Another good business development network is Business Networks International (URL: http://www.bnetal.com).

ONLINE PARTNERSHIPS

The Internet didn't start out as a marketplace; it started out as a collection of individuals, usually computer enthusiasts or academics, who had software programs or information that they wanted to share.

In the past several years, commerce on the Internet has become not only acceptable, but the prevailing culture. However, the core culture of the Internet remains, and that is sharing. This explains one of the current business models on the Internet: partnering. You partner with vendors, with distributors, and sometimes even with your competitors. I provide a link to you on my page, you provide a link to me. We both benefit, we hope.

Edie Davisson says the links page on her site is one of the most popular pages. 'I look on it as an added service to the people who buy my products. If they want to find out more about the botanicals I use, I offer them the links to relevant companies.' She has a reciprocal arrangement with several other companies, where she pays a commission of 10 per cent on sales she makes as a result of referrals. She says that it has worked out well. 'I should say, however, that I know the people I'm dealing with. In this kind of arrangement, you need some trust—but do your homework before you bestow that trust.'

How do you develop a partnership with another company? Col

Jones suggests that you decide what kind of relationship you want, and then you actively search for a company which matches your requirements. Again, you should start with the search engines.

SUPPLIERS

If you're in a service industry, the only supplies you need may be office supplies. However, if you're a manufacturer, you'll need supplies for all your production needs, as well as for equipment. Can you find suppliers on the Internet? Yes! You'll find suppliers both in Australia and overseas. If you do locate an overseas supplier, you'll want to investigate matters such as the cost of shipping, import duty, and perhaps import regulations if you're importing items which are restricted, such as animal products or seeds.

The Internet gives you access to a wide range of resources when it comes to looking for suppliers. You'll find distributors and companies which sell in small quantities. If your needs are for large quantities, you'll also find sites on which you can put out tenders, to make sure that you're getting your materials at the best price possible. Alternatively, your business may entail supplying materials, so you want to locate those businesses which are interested in your products. Or perhaps you're in the business of matching suppliers with companies which need their materials. Contractors and Tenders Worldwide (mentioned later in this chapter) is one of the many sites which allow you to invite tenders.

Finding suppliers on the World Wide Web

If you want to locate suppliers for your trade or industry, your first port of call should be one of the major subject guides, such as Yahoo. This will give you a quick overview of what kind of information is available on suppliers in your area of interest. Depending on the results—if you don't find sufficient information, or if there is too much—try one of the search engines, such as Excite or InfoSeek. SavvySearch is a good option, too, because it allows you to try several search engines at the same time.

Jamie Browne is a purchasing officer for a large Australian company, and she says that the Internet has completely changed the way she does her job; it has made her more effective and productive. 'I save time. I don't need to travel as much as I used to. I'm also dealing with many companies directly rather than going through intermediaries, which helps us to trim our margins.'

Contractors and tenders—worldwide

One way to find companies and individuals to carry out work, or supply goods and services, is to let out tenders. You wouldn't want to let out a tender for every product, or for everything you want to buy; the process takes time. However, many companies never realise that the tendering process is available, and that it can be quite informal. If you deal in tenders (or if you would like to know more about the process), visit URL: http://www.contracts-base.com. The site is well arranged, and well managed.

Here are some reasons you might consider letting out a tender:

- You need a better price than you're getting from your current suppliers.
- You don't know anyone who can supply goods or a service that you need.
- Your suppliers have put their prices up, and you're not sure whether this is feather-bedding or legitimate.
- You're developing a new product or service, and want to know whether you can afford to do it at the price your clients will pay.

Check the FAQ on this site. It gives you all the information you need on how to either invite tenders, or how to bid on a contract. You'll also learn how to create 'open book' tenders, where bidders' questions about your Invitation To Tender, and your answers, can be seen by all bidders—although bidders are identified by reference number only.

Col Jones believes that business-to-business sales on the Web will take off within the next five years. 'I think the Web as a retail business will work for some small business people, but not for all. However, the Web as a way of forming relationships with other businesses, as well as business-to-business sales, that's an area with great potential that people are just now becoming aware of.'

The Internet gives Australian small businesses unlimited expansion capabilities. It's cheap and easy to find overseas companies you want to do business with. Just search for appropriate companies using the search engines, and make a list of prospects. Then find out more about each company by entering a company's name into a search engine—

don't forget to search newsgroup postings as well. After you've checked out a company, send an e-mail message to the principal, introducing yourself, and your business, and include your Web site's URL in your message. Explain your product and how you want to partner with their company, and your relationship will develop from there.

Training and education

Online learning has many benefits, the major one being that it saves time. There's no way you can be an expert in everything, but running a small business requires you to have a knowledge of law, accountancy, marketing, and much more—and of course, you should also be an expert in whatever you happen to be selling. However, your time is at a premium. You could perhaps spare six hours a week to do an accountancy course at TAFE, but when you add travelling time into that equation it becomes impossible. Online learning is very convenient: sit down at your computer, and you're in class. In addition to the time saved, another benefit of online learning is that many courses are free.

The Internet can help you learn whatever you need to run your business successfully. So, what can you learn online? Almost anything, but certainly you'll find many business-related courses, as well as courses which teach you how to make the most of the latest technology. For example, if you want to create your own Web site, you'll find many courses to teach you how to do that. You can also find courses covering many aspects of running a business, such as marketing, accountancy, sales, motivation and time management.

The Internet also puts universities, colleges and libraries at your fingertips. You have access to experts in many fields. You can also search the library catalogues of both Australian libraries and libraries worldwide. Although I haven't provided specific links to many libraries for reasons of space, you should keep your local and state libraries in mind if you're looking for up-to-date information or training material. Libraries have access to a wide range of online resources, such as subscriptions to large (and expensive) international online commercial databases. Through your library, you have free access to these databases. Just ask, and the librarian will perform a search for you in your area of interest.

The training and education sites in the following pages are a sampling to give you an idea what you'll find. The key to using the Internet as a training and educational resource—or any kind of resource, for that matter—is not to assume that the data you want *won't* be available. You'll often be surprised that it is both available and free.

AUSTRALIAN GOVERNMENT EDUCATION AND TRAINING SITES

EdNA— Education Network Australia

URL: http://www.edna.edu.au

EdNA was developed by the Commonwealth government in 1995. It aims to establish a framework for cooperation and collaboration between all sectors of the education and training community, with a focus on information technology. EdNA is a huge database of educational and training resources available both in Australia and overseas. It's an excellent site to use as a starting point, especially if you're not sure of exactly what information is online in your own areas of interest. For example, if you're interested in doing either a university or a TAFE course in small business, you can browse EdNA to see what courses are on offer, and where.

EdNA's aims are:

- to cut down on the frustration of data overload
- to provide authoritative resources for data of many kinds
- to provide pointers to data which are relevant to Australia (when you locate a resource on the World Wide Web there's no way of judging relevancy—EdNA helps you to do that)
- to provide guidelines for organisations for data which will be linked to EdNA for easy access for students as well as the public, and
- to enable data-linking to curricula.

You can either browse EdNA, or use its search function. Information is also available as a hierarchical category tree, similar to Yahoo's system.

Commonwealth Department of Employment, Education, Training and Youth Affairs

URL: http://www.deetya.gov.au
There's a huge amount of information available on this site, and it's also a good place to visit if you're not sure where to find the information you want. You'll find information on many different kinds of training courses; you can advertise your vacancies; and you can also find out the details of the latest government training subsidies, such as the Work for the Dole scheme. Before you write a cheque for a commercial course, whether online or offline, check this site to find out whether you're entitled to any subsidies, or whether you can get the training for free.

Australian Universities online

URL: http://www.avcc.edu.au/avcc/uniwebs.htm
While all Australian universities provide their own Web sites, this page provides links to them on one handy page. Try this page to find an expert in a subject area, or perhaps just find some information or pointers to further training.

Flinders University Library

URL: http://www.lib.flinders.edu.au
Flinders University Library provides free access to many international databases which normally require a subscription. The site is well laid out, and a worthwhile addition to your bookmarks if you're developing your own training course for your staff or yourself. The site also has excellent online Internet tutorials, and other Internet information.

Open Learning Australia

URL: http://www.ola.edu.au
Open Learning Australia provides TAFE, University, and professional and continuing education studies, including many business courses. The courses are inexpensive, and are generally broadcast to students

via radio and television. If this isn't convenient (if the student lives in outback Australia, for example), they are available on video, but at a higher cost. You can sign up for courses via the Web site, or you can make inquiries via e-mail. Complete online courses should be available soon; online support is currently only available for a few courses. The Web site provides other information in addition to course information, such as resources for OLA units and modules, links to Internet resources for the various courses, FAQ files, and more.

Careers Online

URL: http://www.careersonline.com.au/colindex.html
This site provides a lot of good training material free of charge. You can also advertise your vacancies here through the Executive Observation Deck. Careers Online is also an excellent site for job seekers, with good job-hunting information. It's very popular, so you're bound to get a good response to your ads.

IMPROVE YOUR ENTREPRENEURIAL SKILLS

When you run a small business, you not only have to do it all, it's assumed that you have the *know-how* to do it all. In this section, we'll look at World Wide Web sites for the training and education of entrepreneurs. As you'll see, there's a huge amount of information online. You'll need to make a special effort to develop your own study methods to make best use of the information. Try to structure your own training course, as if you were studying at a real college. That is, first collect information on your areas of interest at a number of sites, then divide the information you want to study into modules, and study one module per week, for an hour a day, just as if you were studying at TAFE.

BizTalk

URL: http://www.biztalk.com
BizTalk is an electronic magazine for small business owners. The various departments include news, finance, law, politics and technology. An interesting feature of the site is that BizTalk has contests to provide seed money for start-up businesses. This is an excellent resource to stay abreast of new developments for small business owners.

When last I visited, the online articles included: 'Getting a Great Deal on Equipment Leasing' and 'Productivity Power Tools for Your Small Office'. There's lots of information to improve your skills in many areas.

Idea Café: the small business channel

URL: http://www.ideacafe.com

Idea Café offers a mix of information and fun. They say their aim is to help entrepreneurs succeed in reaching their personal and business goals. You'll find articles on managing your business, and a chat room where you can exchange ideas with others. On the day I visited, there were articles on the millennium bug, wooing venture capitalists, and when to talk money with your clients. Again, there's a lot of information here to hone your skills.

Inc. Online

URL: http://www.inc.com

There's a mass of information on this site. Inc. Online is the Web site of Inc. magazine. You can access online articles published in past issues of the magazine through various databases. It's extremely valuable if you want to bring yourself up to speed on business topics such as marketing, networking and technology for business. Articles in a recent issue included an excerpt from Abraham Maslow's 1962 journals, just published, on what motivates people, and a discussion on 'Am I a boss or a babysitter?', which offers great advice on how to improve your managerial skills.

Marketing Resource Center

URL: http://www.marketingsource.com

This site is a free service of the Concept Marketing Group, Inc. It contains a library of 250 articles on planning and running your business, marketing tools and contacts, as well as a database of industry associations and links to online business magazines. You can register for the free bi-weekly newsletter, which is filled with information and tips. If you have a casual question, you can ask it here in the Marketing Forum. The site also includes free Business Classifieds, if you have anything that you want to buy or sell.

Small Business Advisor

URL: http://www.isquare.com
You'll find a large collection of articles for the new (and experienced) business person on this site. The titles include: 'Don't Make These Business Mistakes', 'Getting Paid', and 'Government Small Business Resources'. There's a free newsletter, business news which is updated daily, marketing tips which are also updated daily, and a lot more which you can find by using the site's search engine.

Small Business Workshop

URL: http://www.sb.gov.bc.ca:80/smallbus/workshop/workshop.html
Although this site is sponsored by the Canadian government, it contains many articles on topics which are relevant to businesses anywhere in the world. The areas covered include: Starting Your Own Business, Marketing Basics, Planning Fundamentals and Financing Your Business, all good information to help you build your business skills.

Skills Online

URL: http://www.skillsonline.com
This is an interesting site devoted to interactive learning. They have a line of educational CD-ROMs, and will also develop courses to your own specifications. They offer online demonstrations of their courses on the site. At this site, the information offered isn't free, but you may find that it's worth paying for.

ONLINE COURSES

Winning with Small Business Course—free online course

URL: http://www.success.org/wwsbc/introduction.html
This online course in managing a small business is completely free, and contains 30 lessons. There's even an exam at the end. Each lesson poses situations, presents ideas, and asks questions. This is designed to get you thinking about your own business, and how to make the ideas work for you in your own situation. Especially valuable are the lessons on writing a business plan, implementing the plan, and redefining your objectives to suit the changing marketplace as you begin to work to the plan.

The best thing about this course (aside from the fact that it's free) is that it's well written in an accessible style which is anything but dry. There's a lot of material: around 300 pages. Aim to treat the course as you would a course at TAFE or some other institution. That is, work through the material at around three lessons a week, devoting at least a couple of hours to each lesson, rather than rushing through it. Highly recommended, especially if you feel as if your business is in a rut. This course will rekindle your enthusiasm.

Beginner's Guide to HTML

URL: http://www.ncsa.uiuc.edu/General/Internet/WWW/HTML Primer.html

Want to create your own Web site? Or perhaps you want to be able to do your own running repairs and adjustments to a site which someone else has created for you. If so, this is the place to start. This free online course teaches you basic Web site development skills. You may find that this material is easier to work with on the Web, rather than from a book, because you can see immediate examples.

ZDnet Learning Online

URL: http://www5.zdnet.com/learning

Try this site if you want to learn how to make the most of your computer and the latest technology. You'll also find business courses here. You'll be charged for any course you take, but most courses are reasonably priced at a fraction of the price of commercial courses. You can also obtain a free trial of whichever courses you're interested in. Courses are scheduled, so you should book. If the course you're interested in has filled—there are only twelve students per course—you can audit that course: that is, you take the course but you don't submit your 'homework'. If you're not sure whether this style of learning is for you, then you can sign up for a free, one-week trial.

LearnItOnline is a part of this site, and this section focuses on interactive computer training over the Internet. It features training in software, such as office suites (database management, word processing and spreadsheets) and graphics. These courses aren't scheduled, so you can begin whenever it suits you.

VIRTUAL UNIVERSITY—FREE

Spectrum Virtual U

URL: http://www.vu.org

Virtual U's virtual campus on the World Wide Web is the largest online learning community on the Internet. Half a million people from 128 countries have attended the online classes. Classes are given by volunteers, and are available at a minimal cost of $US15. If you have expertise in a particular area, and you want to share your expertise with others, you can suggest a subject and develop it into an online course. You'll find courses in many areas: technology, business, humanities, psychology, and more. You can interact with your lecturer and other students in the course via chat rooms.

TRAINING SOFTWARE

WebStudy

URL: http://www.webstudy.com

The WebStudy program supports and enables education and training over the Internet. It allows students from anywhere in the world to access a course using a Web browser. Instructors develop their course's content using standard word processing software.

Finance—your money and your life

Many Australian financial institutions—including stock exchanges, banks, building societies and insurance companies—are online, and provide good information, whether you're a customer or not. However, many of the sites you will probably visit consistently will be in some other part of the world—US newspaper sites, for example, have excellent financial sections. Whatever financial news or services you're interested in, you'll find them somewhere online.

SITES IN AUSTRALIA

Australian Financial Services Directory

URL: http://www.afsd.com.au
This site is currently Australia's largest definitive network of online financial resources. You can access thousands of companies right throughout Australia and worldwide. It also provides links to informational sites such as the Australian Stock Exchange, David Koch's 'My Money' site and Barron's online. This makes it an excellent start for your explorations; chances are, if it concerns money, you'll find a lead on it here.

Included in the directory are: Australian publicly listed companies, the gold mining/resources and precious metals index, stock market and economic reports, charting services, share quotes, data vendors,

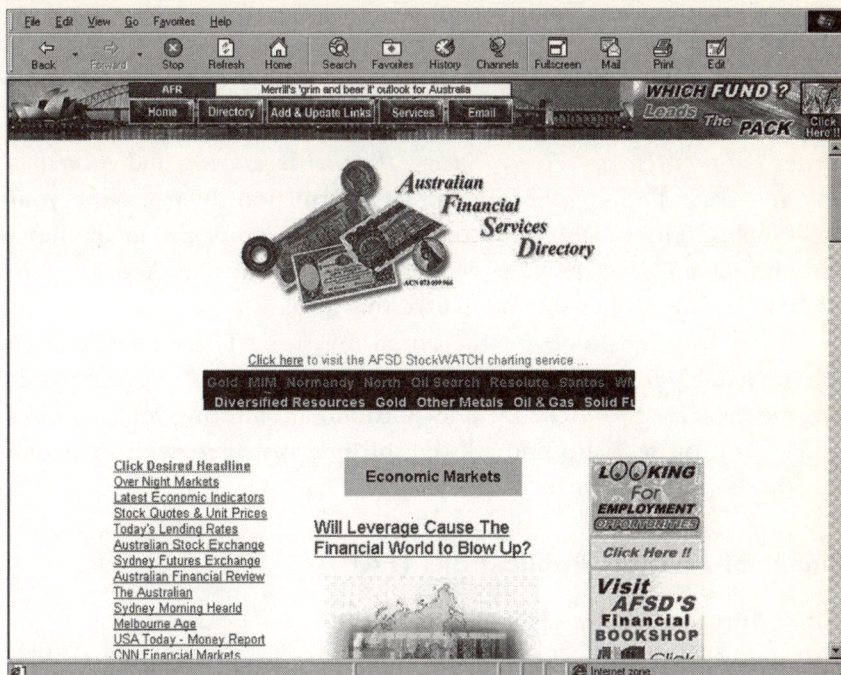

One of the many Australian financial sites on the Web.

fund unit prices, investment forums, taxation advisers, Australian Taxation Office rulings, stock brokers, fund managers, banks, and much more. A section called 'Small Business' provides information for your company; for example, a recent article covered finding sources of venture capital. The site is updated daily.

Australian Stock Exchange

URL: http://www.asx.com.au

Undoubtedly the most important financial site. If you currently own shares, you'll be spending a lot of time here. There's lots of good information for novices as well as seasoned investors. If you're not sure exactly what the stock market is and how it works, you'll find a 'Step by Step Guide to Investing in Shares', which will get you started. There's also a glossary, and a section on finding a stockbroker to handle your investments. The hottest trend for small investors is to do their own share trading online; you can learn to do that too.

Personal Investment

URL: http://www.personalinvestment.com.au

This is the primary site of several magazines covering the financial scene: *Business Review Weekly*, *Shares*, *Personal Investment*, and *Australian Property News*. The site contains lots of information for managing your investments. There's also good information on companies in the news and current financial news, as well as investment advice. You can join readers' forums to get the latest investing tips.

You'll also find 'tools for the wired investor'. These include Web site updates, and software programs to monitor and manage your investments. Free services include portfolio monitoring and a stock-watch list. You will also find a listing of fund managers with their one and three-year performances.

Financial Analysis Publications (FAP)

URL: http://www.financial-analysis.com

This site offers a rival service to the ASX. You'll find company profiles for $2, including brokers' comments. Other services include: company performance reviews for $4 a company; annual company financials for two years for $4; free index cross references; a dividend database ($4 per dividend history since 1985) and capital gains tax data.

PCquote

URL: http://www.pcquote.com

Free price information on US and Australian stocks listed on the New York Stock Exchange. If you want to get started with your own online trading, you'll find the information here. If you want to get started with futures, there's a section of the site which is devoted to them: the Futures Resource Centre. There's a lot of information here, both for the novice and for the professional.

My Money by David Koch

URL: http://www.mymoney.com.au

This is an excellent site if you want the latest financial information in an accessible format. Covers banking strategies, insurance news, and investment and taxation advice.

Australian Financial Review

URL: http://www.afr.com.au

This is the online version of the publication. It features stock tickers with the latest trading figures at the major stock exchanges worldwide, financial news, and editorial material. Most of the site offers free information. However, 'The Trading Room' section does charge for some information. Chargeable information includes real-time share quotes, and archival searches. You're informed when you're about to enter a chargeable area, and while you're in the area, you can keep an eye on what charges you're incurring via a gauge at the bottom of the screen.

Included on the AFR site are:

- Markets: a detailed overview of the Australian share market. 'Market Turnover' shows you what's happening in each of the main segments of the market. 'Market Movers' highlights which stocks are moving, both in the top 100 stocks, and right across the market.
- Investments: helps you to find the stock, managed investment or cash product you're looking for. The Securities section offers various ways to search for stocks. Managed investments' performance data is listed, as are cash investments.
- News: you're shown every announcement to the ASX by every company, in real time. If you want to search the archives, the news archives include news from the *Australian Financial Review*, *BRW Magazine*, *Personal Investment*, *Shares*, the *Sydney Morning Herald* and *The Age*.

Financial Passages Online

URL: http://www.financialpassages.com.au

This site is devoted to helping you make the most of your money, no matter where you are in your career or investment life. You need to join to gain access to the facilities.

AUSTRALIAN BANKS

Many Australian banks (both trading and investment) have an online presence. I've listed a few of them; unless they offer something outstanding, however, I haven't commented on the site. The online services offered vary. Some, such as the Advance Bank, are developing electronic commerce systems. Most will allow you to do your personal banking online, and are developing systems to allow you to conduct your business banking online as well.

Advance Bank

URL: http://www.advance.com.au

Advance offers e-cash, an electronic payment system for the Internet. If you have an account with Advance, you can sign up for e-cash online, and can start spending your electronic dollars in online transactions. Basically, e-cash allows you to make real-time payments of various amounts—as small as one cent. This is very handy for subscriptions to sites which contain information databases, and which require payment for access to full-text articles. However, you can also use e-cash to buy any product or service from merchants who have signed up with the system.

How does it work? As you're browsing the Web, watch for the 'We accept e-cash' symbol; click the appropriate button on the merchant's Web site, and the payment is made immediately, transferring e-cash from a software program called 'Your Purse' (on your PC) to the merchant's e-cash Safe.

Australian and New Zealand Banking Group

URL: http://www.anz.com.au

Colonial State Bank

URL: http://www.sbnsw.com.au

Commonwealth Bank of Australia

URL: http://www.commbank.com.au

The Commonwealth has a large and interesting site, as you might expect. It's also well designed. You can do your online banking on this site; just take the online tour to find out how it works.

Westpac Bank

URL: http://www.westpac.com.au

Westpac has a lot of business information on its site, so it's worth having a look at even if you're not a customer.

INTERNATIONAL FINANCE SITES

The Money Page

URL: http://www.moneypage.com

An excellent site with many features, including a handy feature called 'The Top 10 Banks in Cyberspace'; these are sites which offer Internet banking and bill-paying. Although created for the US, it's a handy site if you do business in the US or if you travel. The site also offers a lot of information about commerce on the Internet and investment.

21st Century Banking Alert Page

URL: http://www.ffhsj.com/bancmail/bancpage.htm

Information on electronic commerce and banking. This site will keep you apprised of current issues and new developments. It also contains a lot of data on the Y2K bug.

USEFUL FINANCIAL SITES

Currency Converter

URL: http://www.oanda.com/cgi-bin/ncc

This site is an interactive Web page, and is designed to allow you to see current conversion rates for 164 currencies. You can convert your money to and from everything from the Albanian lek to the Zambian kwacha, and dozens of currencies in between. You can also check the previous day's rates, or download a customisable currency converter. If you deal with overseas companies, this site is an indispensable resource.

Asia-Pacific Economic Cooperation

URL: http://www.apecsec.org.sg

This organisation is based in Singapore. The Web site carries information on the eighteen member countries' economies, as well as a financial procedures guidebook with government procurement outlines.

India Market Place

URL: http://www.indiaintl.com
This site contains in-depth information on doing business in India. The Indian business news is updated every business day. Additionally, there is extensive information about trade shows being held in India, and links to India-based business management resources, directories and databases, and associations.

Debt collection

URL: http://www.iinet.net.au/~heath/debtbook.html
Debt collection is a problem for all small businesses, especially since commercial debt collection agencies won't handle small accounts. This free online book, written by an Australian for Australian conditions, tells you what debt-collection methods there are, how well (or badly) they work, and how to choose the best method for your situation. If you have outstanding debts, this book may get you on the right track to recovering at least some of your money.

Much of this material comes from behind the scenes: from lawyers, court officials, private investigators and debt collectors. Although the book was published in Victoria in 1990 as *The Debt Book*, much of the information it contains applies generally. You should, however, take the time to learn which laws apply in your state, before you put the advice into action.

Venture Web—Japan

URL: http://www.venture-web.or.jp
If you're searching for a Japanese contact, you should visit this site. You may be looking for a partner in Japan, or considering marketing your products to the Japanese marketplace—whatever your needs, you'll find a connection here. The site also has information on export/import regulations, as well as human resource links.

Web of Culture

URL: http://www.worldculture.com/index.html
Going to a country and don't know the local customs? The Web of Culture is a good place to visit before working with, or travelling to, a new country. The site includes information on business, religious

customs, resources and holidays. Don't miss the amazing page which features images of various gestures and their meanings in different countries.

Government and legal information

The Web provides you with a wealth of government and legal information, with more being made available each month. This may save you hours of waiting on the phone. You may even save yourself some legal fees. It's a good idea to visit your favourite sites once every couple of months, both to see what new information is available and to stay abreast of new and proposed legislation which may affect your business.

GOVERNMENT INFORMATION

Australian government gateway

URL: http://www.fed.gov.au

If you're not sure which area of the government to approach, try this site first. The design is good, and easy to follow. Whether you want the name of your local member, or details on some upcoming legislation, you'll find it here.

It's also a good idea to check out this site if you tender for government contracts, or work with subcontractors who deal with the government. Often you'll find information here which you won't see reported in the media, however the main page of the site also offers quick access to topics which are in the news. For example, on my last visit there was new information flagged on:

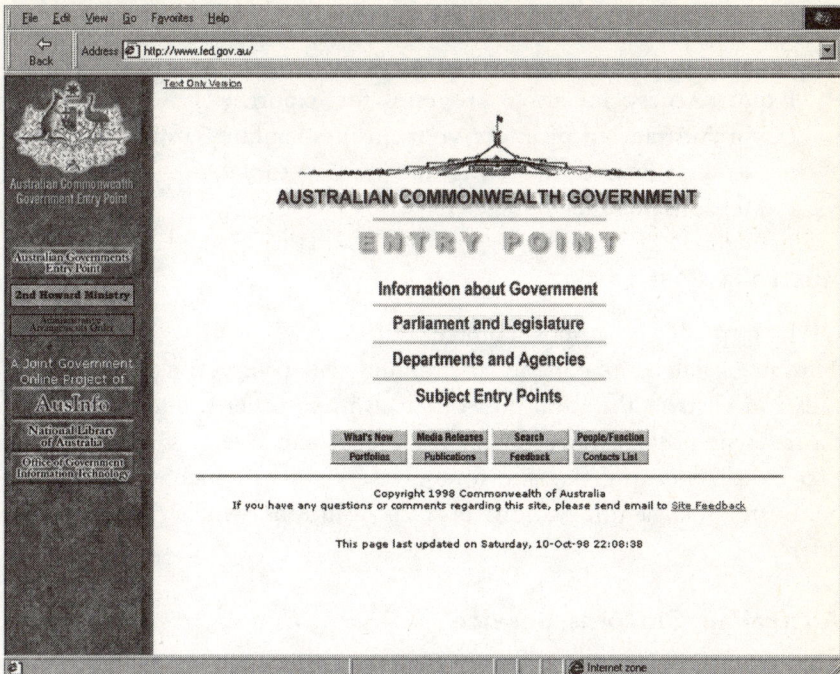

The Australian government gateway.

- The Federal Budget Home Page
- The Department of Veterans' Affairs site
- The High Court of Australia site
- Australian National Audit Office site
- Australian Nature Conservation Agency—Conference List
- National Land Care Program site
- The Salmon Import Risk Analysis Final Report
- Australia's Hong Kong Site

Austrade

URL: http://www.austrade.gov.au

This is a large site, designed both for overseas traders who want to invest in or trade with Australia, and for Australians who want to approach export markets but aren't sure how to get started.

Available areas include:

- Investing in Australia—if your company isn't listed, you can apply for a listing.

- Export Education: investing in overseas markets, with constantly updated information on Asian markets.
- Export Access: incentive programs for export.
- Using Austrade to promote your business online—using the Internet as an effective marketing and trading tool.
- Exhibitions, seminars and events.

Australia Post

URL: http://www.auspost.com.au
This an excellent informational site, and will save you a lot of phone calls and visits to the local post office. Among other things, you'll find the current postage rates for all Australian and overseas mailings. It's also worth checking this site for new services of which you may not be aware, such as the various business solutions which Australia Post offers.

Australian Customs Service

URL: http://www.customs.gov.au
A large and comprehensive site. You should find the answers to all your import/export questions here. Additionally, there are contact phone and fax numbers if you have specific problems.

Australian Securities Commission

URL: http://www.asc.gov.au
This is a valuable site, because it allows you to check the credentials of investment advisers or representatives. The site provides the same checking ability for small businesses, including a list of banned directors. The free information on the site includes company names, ACNs and locations via the National Names Index. If you want to do a full search online, you will need to go through an information broker. Other information includes: how to form a company, how to wind up a company, how to manage insolvency issues, and investing over the Internet.

Australian Taxation Office

URL: http://www.ato.gov.au
This site is continually updated, and changes constantly. However, it

contains instructions on using all sections of the site, so you should find the information you need without too much difficulty.

LEGAL INFORMATION

Australia is a world leader when it comes to providing law content for the Internet. For the small businessperson, information on the international trade laws may be particularly useful. Currently, the Internet and related areas haven't attracted the attention of lawmakers and regulators. However, this won't last forever. As the Internet becomes more important to your business practices, it's a good idea to stay abreast of new developments in this area. Although the vast amount of legal information won't provide you with answers to specific legal problems—don't fire your solicitor—it provides a lot of general information. The value of these sites isn't so much in providing direct answers to your questions, as in giving you enough background so that you know which questions to ask.

Australasian Legal Institute

URL: http://www.austlii.edu.au
This site is the chief source of all primary Australian legal materials on the Web. AustLII is a joint facility of the Faculties of Law at the University of Technology, Sydney (UTS) and the University of New South Wales (UNSW). It gives you access to a plethora of legal material and case information. You can search the databases in a number of ways, including free-form searches.

AustLII currently provides free access to over 2.5 gigabytes of searchable text. This includes legislation, treaties, decisions of courts and tribunals, and secondary materials, including law reform and royal commission reports. The site provides many useful links, including to the Parliament of Australia's Library site (URL: http://library.aph.gov.au/library), which contains transcripts of Bills presented to Parliament, with links to the legislation on AustLII.

ScalePLUS

URL: http://law.agps.gov.au
This is the Federal Attorney-General's Department database of legal

data on the Internet. It includes case law and legislation. It is linked to the Federal Attorney-General's Web site (URL: http://law.gov.au).

International Trade Law

URL: http://itl.irv.uit.no/trade_law
This site is sponsored by the Law Department at Norway's University of Tromso. You can search this site for any subject related to international trade law. Some typical topics include Dispute Resolution, Customs, Protection of Intellectual Property, and various free trade treaties.

National Legal Network

URL: http://www.phone131384.aust.com
The National Legal Network is a network of solicitors in all areas of Australia, any of whom may be reached by a single phone number. The site is quite useful in that, even if the solicitor you want isn't included in their database, they will be able to provide contact details.

Butterworths

URL: http://www.butterworths.com.au
A comprehensive legal site. However, you will need to register, and parts of the site, such as the Lexis-Nexis database, are chargeable. The site includes Legal Express, a daily newsletter which summarises Australian legal news. If you don't choose to register, you will still find a lot of good information here, including many links to other legal sites, as well as government sites.

Law Society of NSW

URL: http://www.lawsocnsw.asn.au
This is a large site, which includes legal news, various resources (all searchable), and a listing of legal firms in New South Wales. There's a lot of free information, the most useful of which is a series of free guides. The topics are many and various. For example, when I visited the site they included how to handle debt problems, handling work injury, and buying a strata unit.

chapter 13

Human resources— hiring on the Net

The Internet is a cost-effective way to hire staff, particularly staff on contracts, whether short or long term. You can also discover what your obligations are as an employer, and can find information to help you design a safer workplace. Teleworking, also known as telecommuting, is becoming popular in many industries; dozens of sites explore the various options, and you can discover whether it's appropriate for your needs.

If you use the Internet, you can save money on hiring staff, because many sites allow you to post job vacancies for free.

HUMAN RESOURCES SITES

Employers' Federation

URL: http://www.employersfed.org.au
This is the most important site to visit if you're thinking of hiring, and all the information is free. The Employers' Federation helps employers with advice on human resources, payroll, industrial relations, and enterprise agreements and awards. It provides publications, seminars and training courses. On the site you'll find information on: awards and payroll (there's information for all employers, both state and federal); the wording of contracts of employment; sample workplace agreements for employers both large and small; employee

dismissals; and general employee management. In addition, you'll find advice for problem solving relevant to your industry, and strategic advice.

Australian Human Resources Institute

URL: http://www.ahri.com.au

The Australian Human Resources Institute is the professional body for people with human resources interests. You can contact the Institute online, and you can read information from *HR Monthly* magazine, which is published by the Institute. You can also become a member, with the benefits of networking at meetings and conferences.

WORKPLACE SAFETY

SafetyLine Workplace Safety

URL: http://www.wt.com.au/~dohswa

This Western Australian site offers workplace safety information which is applicable Australia-wide, as well as information on laws specific to your state. You'll find information on the safe handling of hazardous substances, plant and manual handling safety, noise and work-related illnesses, as well as information on safety issues relevant to specific industries.

Not just a site for those whose jobs deal with safety, there's information here for small business as well. Especially useful is a section on work-related stresses.

SafetySmart.Com

URL: http://safetysmart.com

Another good site with a lot of information, including free reports created for the online audience. SafetySmart.Com was developed by the publishers of *SafetySmart! Magazine*, and as well as free information, you can buy products such as T-shirts, posters and copies of articles published in various media, all with a safety theme. You'll also find links to many other sites concerned with workplace safety.

ADVERTISING YOUR VACANCIES

Aussie Careers Guide

URL: http://www.northnet.com.au/~achamber
This site includes a good search engine. You can advertise your positions here.

JobWeb

URL: http://www.jobweb.com.au
This is a large site with many options. One of the best facilities is the chat option. It also offers an online newsletter.

A Usenet newsgroup for jobs

URL: http://www.aus.ads.jobs
Many people advertise their availability here. If you're looking for someone to do part-time work, you may find a contact. Alternatively, you can advertise the positions you have available.

TELEWORKING

Working from home is becoming more popular in Australia as more employers understand what's involved. If you have a small office, rather than moving you may consider allowing workers to work from home. There are dozens of Internet sites with this theme; the following site gives you an overview of the issues involved.

Telecommuting, Teleworking, and Alternative Officing

URL: http://www.gilgordon.com
This is a site which features telecommuting information from around the world, from many different perspectives. Topics covered include telecommuting, teleworking, the virtual office, and many related topics. It includes a FAQ section and a listing of upcoming events.

Free goodies on the Net

The Internet abounds in free, or *almost* free, goodies. Primary among the goodies is free information.

However, you'll also find a lot of software on the Web, which is either free, or which attracts minimal payment. The 'free' software comes in various varieties:

- Freeware—this software is free for you to use, but the copyright remains with the author. There's a huge amount of freeware on the Internet. The best way to find free programs is to look for them with any search engine: when you find one site which offers freeware, it will give you links to many others, and you'll end up with more software than you'll ever need.
- Shareware—this software is free to download and to try, but at the end of a time period you'll need to pay for it. Shareware is comparable to commercial shrink-wrapped software which you buy at the computer store. However, it often has unique and valuable features which you won't find in commercial products. This is because it's updated more frequently than commercial software. You also have direct contact with the author of the product. If the software doesn't have a feature you need, you can ask for it to be added and the author will usually oblige you. Some business users fight shy of using shareware, thinking that in some way it's inferior to 'proper' software that you buy on the shelf at your

local computer store. But this isn't so—try some of the excellent shareware programs around and prove it to yourself.

- Trialware/demoware—these programs are commercial programs: those which you would buy at your local computer store. However, they're timed versions. This software 'expires' after around a month—it locks, although your data is safe. To be able to continue to use the software, you need to order and pay for the complete version.

Acquiring software over the Internet has these advantages:

- You can see whether the software is what you expected by trialling the product.
- You obtain the latest versions of a product.
- In the case of shareware, you can ask that the product be modified to suit your particular needs—it's a way of gaining customised software cheaply.

FREE INFORMATION—E-ZINES

Electronic magazines abound on the Web. I've listed the top ten e-zines which are currently available. You can subscribe to them very simply by sending messages to the listed e-mail addresses, with 'subscribe' either in the body of the message or in the subject line, as instructed below.

1. All About Biz from AllAboutBiz.com (URL: http://207.226.189.150). Subscribe on the site, or subscribe: Subscribe-3d@allaboutbiz.com
2. The Dollar Stretcher (URL: http://www.stretcher.com). Subscribe on the site. Subscribe: gary@stretcher.com.
3. CyberBiz Newsletter from PoBox.Com (URL: http://www.pobox.com). Subscribe: cyberbiz@pobox.com.
4. Online Business Assistant: Aids, Tips, Tools, Ideas (URL: http://www.finsave.com). Subscribe: imu@finsave.com.
5. The Marketing Coach (URL: http://www.themarketingcoach.com). Subscribe: Leslie@themarketingcoach.com.
6. NetPower New-World Gazette (URL: http://www.powerpub.com). Subscribe: subscribe@powerpub.com.
7. NETResults (URL: http://www.silverquick.com). Subscribe: abnewsman@silverquick.com ('join abnews').

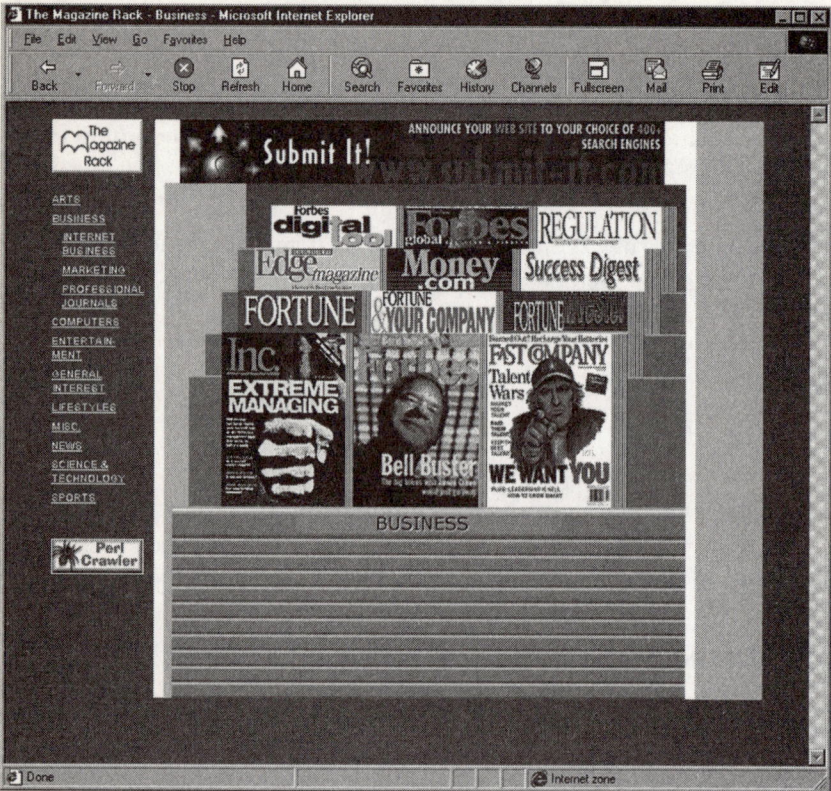

Free online magazines—one of the many free information resources on the Web.

8. Profit 2000 Newsletter (URL: http://www.profit2000.com). Subscribe: Sandy@profit2000.com.

9. Sage Net~Working (URL: http://www.sagewc.com) Julie Frost. Subscribe: enewsletter@sagewc.com.

10. YourHomeBizWeekly (URL: http://www.yourhomebiz.com). Subscribe: subscribeyhbw@yourhomebiz.com.

SOFTWARE—BROWSER PLUG-INS

These utilities are add-ons for your browser. They allow you to watch movies, listen to Internet radio, and more, all through your Internet browser. Browser plug-ins are usually free.

QuickTime by Apple

For: Mac, Power Mac, Windows 95/98/NT
URL: http://quicktime.apple.com
About 70 per cent of all video files on the Internet are in QuickTime format. The files need to be completely downloaded to your computer before you can play them, and are usually one or two megabytes in size. The video appears as a small square in your browser's window, and has controls similar to those on a VCR underneath it. You may already have a version of QuickTime on your computer if you play CD-ROMs. The latest versions are faster, though, and support Quick-Time VR, which is a kind of panoramic photography which you can navigate using your keyboard and mouse.

Shockwave by Macromedia

For: Mac, Power Mac, Windows 95/98/NT
URL: http://www.macromedia.com/shockwave/download
Shockwave files are files created in the program Shockwave Director, using multimedia with embedded links and animations. Shockwave Director allows you to create fancy menus, navigation systems and presentations on your Web site.

RealPlayer by Progressive Networks

For: Windows 95/98/NT, Windows 3.1, Mac, OS2, Linux, Solaris, Sun OS
URL: http://www.real.com/products/player/index.html
RealPlayer uses streaming audio and video. Streaming means that you can play the files while you are still downloading them. There are occasional pauses during which the player buffers more information before playing it. There are many RealAudio and RealVideo sites on the Internet.

Crescendo by Live Update

For: Mac, Windows
URL: http://www.liveupdate.com/midi.html
A plug-in which allows you to insert MIDI files into your Web site. The files play when a visitor accesses the site.

Acrobat by Adobe

For: Mac, Windows, Linux, Aix
URL: http://www.adobe.com/proindex/acrobat/readstep.html
You can download the Acrobat reader, which decodes PDF (Portable Digital Format) files. PDF files are common across the Internet because they enable you to retain the exact format and layout of files. They are also searchable, print on any printer, and can include hyperlinks. If you go to the Australian Senate site, you can read Hansard in PDF format each sitting day.

Pointcast Network by Pointcast Corporation

For: Power Mac, Windows 95/98/NT
URL: http://www.pointcast.com
Pointcast downloads information to your computer. You can personalise it, choosing areas such as general news, weather, sports and information technology news. Abstracts of items appear on your desktop, and the program acts as a screensaver when you're not using your machine. Each item includes hyperlinks, so if you want more information you can click on a link and it will access the site via your browser.

SOFTWARE—INTERNET UTILITY PROGRAMS

The programs below are either free, or available at minimal cost. For a huge selection of free software, both for business and personal use, try URL: http://www.completelyfreesoftware.com.

Data Grabber (free)

Requirements: PC, Windows 95/98
URL: http://www.wildcowpublishing.com/datagrab.html
Data Grabber does exactly what its name suggests. It's a desktop search tool, targeting around 300 public databases on the Internet. When you run the program, its icon sits in your search tray. Simply click on the icon and enter your search terms, then select where you'd like to search. You can select from individual search engines, parallel search engines, or specialised search engines for images, as well as lots of other databases. This brilliant program will save you hours of Internet searching. It's now in version 3, and is often updated.

Web Turbo (free)

Requirements: Windows 95/98
URL: http://www.webturbo.com
Web Turbo integrates itself into your browser; when you install it you'll see its name on your browser's title bar—just click to activate the program. It makes finding, viewing and organising information on the Web much simpler and faster. Web Turbo splits your browser screen in two, and when you type a search query into the Web Turbo window, Web Turbo queries six search engines and presents the results as a 'hypersketch' outline, summarising the pages that it has found. Simply surf through these previews of the information—no need to load the Web pages themselves. This makes finding the information you need much faster. You can even save the outlines that Web Turbo has created for you in order to use them again. Although the program sounds complex, it's amazingly easy to use. There's even a tutorial movie to get you started.

CyberContact Light (free)

Requirements: Windows 95/98
URL: http://www.liraz.com/cybercontact
CyberContact is a PIM (Personal Information Manager) which focuses on your Web-related contact information. It's indispensable if you use your online sessions to manage your business. You can use it to manage all your Web data, including e-mail, tasks, appointments and activities, URLs, Web pages, documents and files. The program's special features include: the ability to file e-mail with your contacts, send e-mail and browse the Web directly from the program, send broadcast e-mail, and manage your tasks and activities. This freeware version allows you 100 contacts in two files. If you need more, upgrade to the Pro version.

NetClipper ($32)

Requirements: Windows 95/98
URL: http://home.jps.net/csware
NetClipper is a simple program—it saves time by allowing you to grab the locations of downloads, for downloading at a later time. You can make your lists of downloads, and then work at something else while the files are downloaded. It works with both Netscape Navigator and

Microsoft Internet Explorer. NetClipper handles any kind of download: files, Web pages, graphics, etc.

WebTabs ($45)

Requirements: Windows 95/98
URL: http://www.hotfiles.com
WebTabs is much more than a URL manager: it also monitors your actions on the Web. It creates bookmarks automatically as you visit sites, tracks the URLs you visit repeatedly and encourages you to annotate them, supports drag and drop for organising your bookmarks, cross-references folders and bookmarks, supports various search options, and allows you to export your collections as HTML files. The windowed interface is simple to use, and allows you to see all your information at a glance.

Calypso Mail (Lite version free)

Requirements: Windows 95/98
URL: http://207.115.144.206/index.htm
Calypso is an ideal e-mail client for SOHO and corporate users. It features an Explorer-style interface, and provides support for multiple accounts. The program is easy to set up—most of the work is done via a Wizard. Some of Calypso Mail's sophisticated features include: automatic reply, auto spell-check, multiple signatures, filtering, bulk e-mail, templates, and fast retrievals. A complete online Help system is provided.

WebExpress ($100)

Requirements: Windows 95/98
URL: http://www.mvd.com
This program gives you a complete Web-authoring tool in a program which is as easy to use as your word processor. Its focus is on your complete Web site, rather than on individual pages. It visually tracks pages in your site and how they are linked; just double-click, and you can open the page for editing. The program remembers which site you worked on last, and which files were open and closed; it also includes Web site image maps. It has all the latest features—you can

create frames and forms, and you can even edit Javascript and VBScript from within the program.

FTP Explorer (free)

Requirements: Windows 95/98
URL: http://www.ftpx.com
This brilliant program makes transferring files to a remote computer as easy as copying files on your home machine. Some of the many clever features include: the ability to download or upload files to one or more servers while browsing, or choosing files to transfer on another; automatic retry, if your connection attempt fails; support for resuming interrupted file transfers; and full drag and drop support.

CyberSense Personal Search (free)

Requirements: Windows 95/98
URL: http://www.cybersense.com/search
This program is a free search engine control centre, and you can install it in your favourite browser. The program's main feature is Quick Search, which lets you send your search query to your choice of nine of the most popular search engines, including AltaVista and Yahoo. The program offers various customisation features via Javascript and cookie technology. The best way to use the program is to make it the home page in your browser. Full instructions on using Personal Search are included on a HTML page; simply open the page in your browser to install the program.

ClickMail 32 (free)

Requirements: Windows 95/98
URL: http://datastod.simplenet.com/ClickMail32.htm
Why bother loading a large program just to send your e-mail? Let ClickMail 32 send it for you—the program dials up your e-mail connection, sends your mail, and then disconnects. Install the program into the directory in which you intend to keep it; there's no set-up program. When you start it, you're given the option of whether you want to make it your default mailer.

FindNews ($8)

Requirements: Windows 95/98
URL: http://www.planetarium.com

This tiny program is a handy Usenet utility. It installs itself into the menu bar of your default newsreader, and allows you to search news headers for specific words or phrases. A great timesaver if you regularly monitor heavy-traffic groups, and don't want to scroll through all the headers.

NewsFerret (free)

Requirements: Windows 95/98
URL: http://www.ferretsoft.com/netferret/sales.htm

NewsFerret is one of the many free Internet utilities produced by the Ferretsoft company. This program installs itself onto your desktop; when you need some information which you think may be available in a newsgroup, just click to start the program, and enter your query—it will even load your dialer for you if you don't have a direct connection. You can enter as many keywords as you like to cut down on the irrelevant matches that you find. You can also speed up searching by limiting the number of results.

WebFerret (free)

Requirements: Windows 95/98
URL: http://www.ferretsoft.com

WebFerret is a delightful free tool which queries a number of the largest Web search engines in order to locate the information you want. The search engines include AltaVista, Euroseek, Yahoo, LookSmart and Lycos. WebFerret queries all its configured search engines simultaneously, and discards duplicate results. Your results start to come back within a couple of seconds, so you can surf directly to the sites WebFerret has located without wasting any time. It's your choice how many results you want located: for example, you can opt for 500 results in total for all the engines, or 500 results per engine. When you type your keywords into WebFerret's query box, you're given a choice of whether you want Web pages to include all the keywords, or any keyword you've entered, so you can narrow your search. The program's best feature is speed: WebFerret will save you serious time on the Web.

Internet EZ Search ($25)

Requirements: Windows 95/98
URL: http://www.americansys.com
EZ Search also speeds up your Internet searching: it lets you query up to 39 search engines at once and it will even remove any duplicate results for you. The program couldn't be easier to use. Simply enter your search terms into the box, then tick off the search engines you want to use on the left. Clever features include: the ability to verify that links are still operational, the ability to view results as a Web page, and in-context Help.

The Web Promotion Spider (free)

Requirements: Windows 95/98
URL: http://www.inthetriangle.com/spider
Although it's best to register your Web site with the major search engines manually, you'll find that it's too much trouble to bother with the hundreds of smaller search engines—you could spend weeks doing nothing else. This is where the Web Promotion Spider is so useful. It registers your site with all those 'other' search engines—almost 300 of them.

The registration process is very simple. You fill in a number of blank fields in separate windows in the application. The information which is required is the URL of the site you want to list, several keywords, a site description, the category you want to be listed under, and the search engines with which you want to register. Once you've entered all the information, click the button and the program contacts each search engine and sends the information for you.

GIF Construction Set ($25)

Requirements: Windows 95/98/NT
URL: http://www.hotfiles.com
Animated GIFs are graphics which can jazz up a static Web page—an animated GIF is simply a number of images played in sequence, thus giving the impression of motion. They give your site visual interest

without requiring you to invest in large expensive programs such as Macromedia Flash or Director. Animated GIFs are most popular as the animated icons for e-mail links, banner ads and menus. Using Mindwork's GIF Construction Set, you can string together a set of images, creating your own animation. The program is simple to use, and allows you to create various other effects in addition to animation.

Shopping Cart ($250)

Requirements: Windows 95/98/NT
URL: ftp://www.webgenie.com/pub/wsc32.exe
You can download this program for free, and try it for 30 days to see whether it works on your site. It's a real bargain when you consider that its commercial cousins sell for thousands of dollars, and you can't try them out first. Basically, this program turns your site into an interactive shop; it allows you to make sales online. All you need to do is to enter your products, descriptions, and the prices. Standard Web pages are created automatically, and you can adapt them to include your company logo, other graphics, and whatever additional information you want to include. The orders are processed via e-mail, although you can modify this option if you wish.

Neoplanet (free)

Requirements: Windows 95/98/NT
URL: http://www.download.com
Neoplanet is a small, free Web browser which does most of what the large browsers do, including receiving and sending e-mail. Its best feature is its small size. If you're working on a notebook computer, it's ideal. It offers channels up-front, as well a built-in Web directory to make locating your favourite Web sites easier. You can customise the program to complement the way you like to work. Extremely handy is the inclusion of the Alexa navigation tool's What's Related feature, which shows you pages similar in content to the page you're currently viewing. This is the first release of Neoplanet to include an integrated e-mail client, and a modem speed booster for faster page downloads.

Alexa Internet (free)

Requirements: Windows 95/98/NT
URL: http://www.alexa.com
Alexa is a free Web site navigation service with unique and useful features. If you're concerned at the amount of time you spend on the Web, Alexa can make that time more valuable. Alexa gives you pertinent details about any Web site you're currently browsing: the registered owner of the site, the number of pages, the freshness of the pages, the loading speed, and more. It can also provide you with a list of similar sites; this is based on the Web surfing habits of other Alexa users. You can also vote on any site, giving it a bouquet or a brickbat, to guide other Alexa users in their explorations. Perhaps the best feature is Alexa's ability to store sites, so that if you click on a page which is unavailable, Alexa can deliver the page directly from its online archive.

(appendix 1)

Online basics—what you need

Although it's a public network, many smaller private networks are part of the Internet. Gaining 'Internet access' basically means hooking your computer into this world network. To take your business online you need:

*   Hardware: a computer; a modem (a device for adding communication abilities to your computer via your phone line).
*   Internet access, through an ISP (Internet Services Provider).
*   A POP (Post Office Protocol) e-mail account.
*   Software: an e-mail client, and a Web browser (software to read documents and view graphics on the Web).

COMPUTER HARDWARE

The right computer

You need a computer, of course. Preferably a PC, capable of running Windows 98, rather than a Macintosh. Not because PCs are better—in fact Macintoshes are superior machines in many ways to PCs—but simply because you'll be limited as far as software is concerned if you have a Macintosh. There's much more software available for PCs, and since most other users will be running PCs it makes communicating and sharing information in the connected world much easier if you're using the same software. This doesn't mean that if you own a Mac you need to throw it out, but you should be aware that your online life will be easier with a PC, and take that into consideration when you upgrade.

Although your computer doesn't need to be the latest, most powerful machine available, it does need to have plenty of RAM (Random Access Memory). Each program you run—and when you go online you'll be running at least three programs, often as many as six—needs memory. To minimise crashes, and a machine which runs like molasses, aim for around 128 megabytes of RAM.

The right modem

A modem is the hardware you need to hook your computer into your phone line so you can dial into your ISP. This is a machine that lets your computer communicate with other computers over the phone lines. Since 1996, most new computers are sold with built-in modems. You may not be aware that you own a modem, because modems come in two varieties—built-in and external. If your computer has a built-in modem, you won't see it, so you won't know that it's there. To check whether your machine has a modem, look at the documentation which came with your computer, and read the specifications. You can also call the people who sold you the machine, and ask them whether the machine has a modem.

Your modem choices

For business use, a 33.6 modem is an adequate and affordable choice. If you have a reasonably fast PC, with around 64 megs of RAM, you'll be able to create your own Web site, and browse the Web comfortably. The next step up is a 56K modem. However, because you're still trying to squeeze a lot of digital data through a narrow pipe, you won't get 100 per cent improvement over a 33.6 modem. For small businesses, say with from one to five employees, 33.6 to 56K modems are recommended.

However, to be comfortably running your larger small business online, or if your entire business consists of an online enterprise, you should opt for an ISDN connection. An ISDN (Integrated Services Digital Network) connection basically means that you're using digital phone lines, rather than analogue. An ISDN connection means you'll need to do a little more research to find the right provider. There's also a learning curve, and some hassle in setting up the service, but once that's done it's both fast and fun. With an ISDN line, you'll be able to conduct all the telecommunications for your business over a single line, although it does mean that you'll have more than one phone number. Your voice, fax and data transmissions all go over a single digital line, with different numbers.

ISDN is not cheap. It's a double hit. You'll pay Telstra for the use of the line (say goodbye to untimed phone calls), and you'll also have to pay an ISP for Internet access. However, if your Web site becomes an important part of your business, and you make a lot of sales via the site, an ISDN line makes good sense. Justin Magnan, the President of inkjetrefills.com (http://www.inkjetrefills.com) operates his business solely via the Internet. He uses ISDN to satisfy corporate and private customers all over the world, and is very happy with the ISDN system.

AFFORDABLE DIAL-UP CONNECTIONS

Let's go into a little more detail about your Internet connection options. You have three main options. These are:

- a modem with a dial-up Internet connection;
- a modem with a permanent Internet connection;
- an ISDN connection.

There are other options, however these are used by large corporations, and are too expensive to be practical for a small business person. Which one is for you?

A modem with a dial-up connection

Hop over to the nearest computer superstore, grab a modem, connect it to your office PC, and plug into your phone line. Within an hour or so, you're in business on the Internet. It's fast, it's simple, and it's easy. It's the ideal way for the new business user to discover what the Internet has to offer. You have no ongoing charges, other than to your ISP. However, the problem with a dial-up connection is that you need to dial into your ISP each time you want to use the Internet.

A modem with a permanent connection

Most ISPs will give you the option of a permanent modem connection. Basically, this means that you pay for the use of a modem at the provider's end—so there are no busy signals when you dial in to your ISP. This is a good solution for many small businesses, and you'll probably need a permanent modem connection when you have your own Web site set up. Charges for this service vary. An average price would be $200 and upwards for setting up the service. You will also be charged for the amount of traffic flowing to your site, usually per gigabyte, with a monthly minimum charge. Count on $300 and upwards per month.

An ISDN connection

This is where the plot thickens. An ISDN is a high-speed permanent connection to the Internet. You'll be paying out to Telstra, as well as to your ISP, and you'll need Telstra to set up the service for you. If you're interested in an ISDN connection, check with Telstra first; ISDN is not available in all areas. Telstra offers an excellent explanation of what ISDN is, and how it works, complete with diagrams—so check out www.telstra.com.au.

If you acquire an ISDN connection, all your office communications will work via ISDN. The channels vary, according to what you purchase from Telstra, but a basic connection allows you to connect your phones, your fax machines, and data transmission devices (computers) to the ISDN line. ISDN works at around twice the speed of the fastest available modems. You could use ISDN for:

- Telephony: ISDN gives you a minimum of two phone connections to a maximum of eight phone connections. You will thus have separate numbers for phones, faxes and computers, which will be programmed into the equipment. You can add your PABX to the service.
- Data transfer: you can send data from one computer to another—such as text files, spreadsheets, graphics, etc.
- Faxing, including high-speed colour faxing.
- Internet access, especially ultra-speedy World Wide Web access.
- Telecommuting: instant access to head office, or outlying branches.
- Videoconferencing: two-way audio and video.

If you're considering ISDN, you should be aware that the service is not available in all areas. Your local exchange must have ISDN equipment installed—check with Telstra. Also, you need to be within 3.5 to 4.5 kilometres of your local phone exchange.

Check whether your current office PCs can handle high-speed data transmission; older PCs may not be able to handle it:

- You will need to buy a Terminal Adaptor or ISDN card for your PC; think of these devices as an ISDN modem.
- You'll need to check whether your analogue phones will work with the Terminal Adaptor or ISDN card you've chosen; if you have an older fax, you should also check that it will work with ISDN.
- Your ISDN numbers will be different from your old numbers, therefore you will need to advertise your new phone and fax numbers. You can have a diversion placed on your old numbers.
- ISDN is not portable. If you move your business, you will need to pay for reconnection—provided that the service is available in the area you are moving to.

Upcoming Internet technologies

Chief among the emergent Internet technologies are cable modems, and various other kinds of transmissions, including via satellite. This area of telecommunications is so volatile that prediction on what will be available within a year or two is useless. When you're ready to put your business online, use the same commonsense that you use in other areas of your business. Don't be on the bleeding edge of technology, and don't believe promises of salespeople or technology developers. Make sure that any technology you intend using in your business is proven, and that it is currently being used by thousands of other people.

E-mail software

You'll be spending a lot of time with your e-mail program, so choose wisely. Most business users seem to spend around half an hour a day writing, replying and reading their messages, so the best e-mail program is the one which does what you want simply and easily. The platform you're using (Windows, Apple, DOS, OS2) determines which programs you can use. If you're running Windows, you have a great number of options. Comprehensive e-mail programs, such as Qualcomm Systems' Eudora, have much the same functions as Outlook 98. The features your e-mail software should have include:

1. An address book which interfaces with other programs on your computer, such as your word processor. You'll often want to send a letter to someone who has contacted you via e-mail. It's handy if you can just click on a menu option which says something like 'Send letter to contact', and have your word processor start with the contact's name and address already inserted. Your e-mail program's address book should definitely have Internet functionality: that is, you should be able to store e-mail addresses and URLs in the program.

2. Easy contact management. For example, Outlook can create a contact from any e-mail message you receive. You right-click on the sender's e-mail address, and choose 'Create Contact'. A record is created for the contact. Or, you can simply drag a message to Outlook's Tasks list, and a new task is created for the contact. If you want to create an appointment for the contact, you drag the message to the Calendar. Most high-end mail programs have similar features.

3. A way to store messages simply so that you can find them again. It's frustrating to click your way through months of e-mail messages to find a message you know is there somewhere. Your e-mail software should have a method for searching through all the e-mail messages you've received.

4. The ability to send attachments. You'll often want to send a document to someone, so your software should have an 'attach file' option. For example, you may want to send a prospect your product brochure, or a price-list.

5. Your software should provide an option which lets you screen out messages coming from certain people and organisations: a 'junk' filter. This feature of your mail program intercepts messages you've designated as 'junk', the electronic equivalent of junk mail. If you're a heavy user of e-mail, you can end up receiving hundreds of messages a day, and many of these will be unwanted messages— such as advertising from people who've managed to get hold of your e-mail address. Junk filters usually work by storing messages

you've designated as junk in a Junk folder; you can delete these messages manually, or have the program do it automatically. A warning about junk filters: they are not perfect, so don't set the filter to automatically 'delete'. It's best to scan the contents of your junk folder before you delete the messages. You might find that the program has somehow managed to junk an important message from a client (or worse, from your boss).

6. Automatic features. Aside from junk filters and distribution lists, many e-mail programs have features which allow you to set automatic responses to certain messages, usually messages which are addressed in a particular way. For example, you could have your program set to automatically send your price list to all messages addressed to info@yourcompany.com.au. Read the manual, or the Help file of your program, to discover what other automatic features your program has.

Additional resources

MAGAZINES AND NEWSPAPERS ONLINE

Citysearch Australia from the Sydney Morning Herald

URL: http://www.citysearch.com.au
A good starting place if you want to know what's happening in your local area. The local information includes events, restaurants, cafes, movies, local organisations and sporting events in a calendar format. Citysearch covers Sydney, Melbourne and the world, via Citysearch Worldwide. Especially useful is the Business to Business section; depending on what your business is, you might consider advertising here.

Advertising Age

URL: http://www.adage.com
One of the most useful areas of the Advertising Age site is a section called NetMarketing, which focuses on getting the most out of your Web site. Another useful section is DataPlace, which features a big collection of industry reports and statistics.

Barron's Online

URL: http://www.barrons.com
This useful site contains the complete contents of their weekly

publication. It also features the ability to examine most companies mentioned in their articles through a resource called the Barron Dossiers. Barron's Online requires registration, but the registration is free.

BusinessWeek

URL: http://www.businessweek.com
This large site includes a lot of information which is only available online. For example, the online version includes Maven, the interactive computer shopper, and BW Plus, which contains business book reviews, articles on the computer industry and articles on information technology. You can also try BW Radio, which provides hourly market reports in RealAudio format (download and install the free plug-in first).

Entrepreneurial Edge Online

URL: http://www.edgeonline.com
Lots of general business information, including a Pointers from the Pros section, SmallBizNet (with a full digital library), and also the Interactive Toolbox, a series of self-calculating worksheets and benchmarking and assessment tools.

Entrepreneur Magazine Online

URL: http://www.entrepreneurmag.com/entrepreneur.hts
This is the online version of *Entrepreneur* magazine, and you'll find a mass of small business information on topics such as money, technology, business management, marketing, and new opportunities. It's worth checking this site on a monthly basis, if the mix of information appeals to you—or you can join their mailing list and get free notification of updates to the site.

Fast Company

URL: http://www.fastcompany.com
Fast Company is a new business magazine with lots of articles on all kinds of business situations. The articles all have an edge; there's very little sugar-coating of unpleasant realities. This is the online version; it includes most of the articles found in the print version.

Financial Times (US)

URL: http://www.usa.ft.com

This site features various sections of the US print publication, including News & Comment. It also contains abstracts of articles from the print version, stock market info which is updated every 30 minutes, Themes and Topics (categorised articles); and other useful information.

Forbes Digital Tool

URL: http://www.forbes.com

In addition to current and archived articles from *Forbes*, there's the Toolbox, a collection of reports and indices; ASAP, Forbes' supplement on information technology; Angles, a section on media and politics; and there's also access to a free resource called the Investment Monitor.

Fortune

URL: http://www.pathfinder.com/fortune

This site features areas dedicated to the stock market, mobile computing, managing your money, and information technology. You'll also find a special Fortune Forum for exchanging views on investing with others—you could pick up some handy tips.

The Sydney Morning Herald

URL: http://www.smh.com.au

Don't have time to read a real newspaper? You get the best of SMH online. Sections include News, Icon (technology), Drive (cars) and Jobs.

MARKETING RESOURCES

American Demographics/Marketing Tools

URL: http://www.marketingtools.com

At this site, you can check current consumer trends, as well as the latest tactics and techniques for information marketers. The site also contains Forecast, a newsletter of demographic trends and market forecasts.

American Marketing Association

URL: http://www.ama.org
AMA is an organisation for marketing professionals as well as for small business. Their Web site features a special section on Internet marketing ethics, as well as other useful information on marketing on the Internet.

Business Intelligence Centre

URL: http://future.sri.com
How much do you know about your customers? There's a lot of information on this site about how to gather market research, which makes it an excellent resource for small business people.

Business Wire

URL: http://www.businesswire.com
Business Wire is a leading source of news on major US companies, including the Fortune 1000 and NASDAQ companies. You can look up a company, category, keyword or region for business news.

Selling.com

URL: http://www.selling.com
Although this site is for salespeople, we all sell, and you'll improve your results here. The site contains a collection of selling concepts and exercises.

SOHO (SMALL OFFICE HOME OFFICE) RESOURCES

American Express Small Business Exchange

URL: http://www.americanexpress.com/smallbusiness
Although this is a US site, you'll find a lot of useful information on it. There's a section where you can ask for help from experts in any area in which you're interested, plus you can check out the archives for questions which have already been answered. There's also a tip of the month, and a planning and resources section with information on starting, managing or expanding your business.

Bathrobe 'til 10

URL: http://www.slip.net/~sfwave
Lots of articles and information for self-employed people.

BizProWeb

URL: http://www.bizproweb.com
Everything for small business. There's a mass of articles here from business experts, as well as links to new small business Web sites and software for small businesses to download.

Biz$hop

URL: http://www.bizshop.com
A good site for entrepreneurs. You'll find lots of reports and free business resources here. For example, there's a free report called 'First 25 Business Decisions', which is valuable if you're going it alone. For novices, one of the best sections is the 'Net Profits Tour': how to start making money online.

BizResource.com

URL: http://www.bizresource.com
Another site for small business people and entrepreneurs. BizResource includes a series of business tips (available both via e-mail and online), as well as a business chat area and a series of audio, video and computer resources. The site is updated weekly, so you'll always find new material here.

Business@Home

URL: http://www.gohome.com
The site's motto is 'Making a Life While Making a Living', which covers the eclectic mix of material you'll find. A great feature is an electronic magazine for the growing numbers of people working from home. It includes articles on combining your working space with your living space, time management, marketing and technology. The Cool Tools area reviews recent hardware and software valuable for the general home office worker, while the Consultant's Corner focuses on advice for consultants working from home.

Home Office Links

URL: http://www.ro.com/small_business/homebased.html
You can use this site as a jumping-off point to small and home-based business information on the Web. There's a mass of links, including franchises, business opportunities, reference material, newsgroups, searching tools, and much more. If it concerns small business, you'll find a link to it here.

Your Small Office

URL: http://www.smalloffice.com
This site is the online version of *Small Office Computing* and *Home Office Computing* magazines. It features articles from the print publications, as well as additional resources for online visitors. There's a mass of reviews of network, computer and office equipment, plus a large 'How To' section covering the gamut of small business concerns, from starting a business to finances, and sales and marketing.

Internet Service Providers in Australia

Your ISP controls your Internet experience. Finding the right one for you means finding a provider with the right mix of price and service to suit your requirements. The larger ISPs, which charge by the hour, provide a slightly higher level of service. You won't experience busy signals when you try to log on, for example. However, if you use the service every day, those hourly charges can quickly mount up.

Keep phone charges in mind. If you live in a large city, you'll be able to find many providers which you can access via a local call. If you live in the country, you may not be able to get local call access.

The easiest way to find a provider in your area is to look in your Yellow Pages directory, or look through one of the Australian Internet magazines. The following list gets you started. However, it's by no means a definitive listing—there are many hundreds of ISPs in Australia.

Access One Tel: 1800 818 391 Email: info@aone.net.au
Areas covered: Adelaide, Brisbane, Bundaberg, Cairns, Canberra, Darwin, Gold Coast, Hobart, Latrobe Valley, Mackay, Melbourne, Newcastle, Perth, Rockhampton, Sunshine Coast, Sydney, Toowoomba, Townsville.
APANA Tel: (02) 9635 1751 Email: info@apana.org.au
Areas covered: Melbourne, Sydney.
Auslink Communications Tel: (02) 9232 1381
Email: sales@auslink.net
Areas covered: Adelaide, Brisbane, Melbourne, Perth, Sydney.

AUSNet Tel: 1800 806 755 Email: sales@world.net
Areas covered: Adelaide, Brisbane, Canberra, Darwin, Melbourne, Perth, Sydney.
CompuServe Pacific Tel: 1300 555 520
Email: 70006.101@compuserve.com
Areas covered: Adelaide, Brisbane, Canberra, Darwin, Gold Coast, Hobart, Melbourne, Newcastle, Perth, Sydney.
Connect.com.au Tel: 1800 818 262
Email: connect@connect.com.au
Areas covered: Adelaide, Brisbane, Canberra, Geelong, Gold Coast, Hobart, Melbourne, Nambour, Newcastle, Perth, Sydney, Townsville, Wollongong. Also offers extended calling areas (local call access) around Melbourne and Sydney.
Dialix Tel: 1902 29 2004 Email: info@dialix.com.au
Areas covered: Adelaide, Bribie Island, Caboolture, Camden, Campbelltown, Canberra, Gosford, Karuah, Melbourne, Mulgoa, Nelson Bay, Newcastle, Penrith, Perth, Raymond Terrace, Redcliffe, Samford, Sydney, Tea Gardens, Windsor, Wisemans Ferry.
Frontier Touring Co Tel: 1800 809 164
Email: info@frontiertouring.com.au
Areas covered: Adelaide, Albury, Bairnsdale, Ballarat, Brisbane, Bundaberg, Cairns, Canberra, Darwin, Geelong, Gosford, Hamilton, Hobart, Launceston, Maroochydore, Melbourne, Mildura, Moe, Perth.
GigaNet Tel: 1800 686 884 Email: enquiry@giga.net.au
Areas covered: Adelaide, Albury-Wodonga, Ballarat, Brisbane, Camden, Campbelltown, Canberra, Geelong, Gold Coast, Gosford, Griffith, Helensburgh, Hobart, Junee, Melbourne, Mulgoa, Nambour, Newcastle, Penrith, Perth, Sydney, Townsville, Wagga Wagga, Windsor, Wisemans Ferry, Wollongong.
Harvey Norman Tel: 1800 809 164
Email: info@harveynorman.com.au
Areas covered: Adelaide, Albury, Bairnsdale, Ballarat, Bendigo, Brisbane, Bundaberg, Cairns, Canberra, Darwin, Geelong, Gosford, Hamilton, Hobart, Launceston, Maroochydore, Melbourne, Mildura, Moe, Perth, Rockhampton, Rosebud, Sale, Shepparton, Southport, Sydney, Toowoomba, Townsville, Wangaratta, Whyalla, Wodonga, Wollongong.
Hutchison Telecommunications Tel: 133 488
Email: info@hutch.com.au
Areas covered: Adelaide, Brisbane, Melbourne, Perth, Sydney.

IBM Global Network Tel: 132 426
Email: inetinfo@vnet.ibm.com
Areas covered: Adelaide, Ballarat, Brisbane, Canberra, Hobart, Melbourne, Newcastle, Perth, Sydney, Wangaratta, Wollongong, and local POPs in 50 countries.

Internet Access Australia Tel: (03) 9686 6677
Email: iaccess@iaccess.com.au
Areas covered: Adelaide, Axedale, Ballarat, Bendigo, Bridgewater, Brisbane, Canberra, Central Coast, Geelong, Gold Coast, Goornong, Harcourt, Laanecoorie, Melbourne, Perth, Sydney.

Magna Data Tel: 1300 262 036 Email: sales@magna.com.au
Areas covered: Brisbane, Melbourne, Sydney, Wollongong.

Microplex Tel: (02) 9438 1234 Email: info@mpx.com.au
Areas covered: Adelaide, Albury, Armidale, Bathurst, Brisbane, Bundaberg, Campbelltown, Canberra, Dalby, Darwin, Gosford, Gunnedah, Gympie, Hobart, Katoomba, Kingaroy, Lismore, Mackay, Maryborough, Melbourne, Moree, Narrabri, Nowra, Orange, Penrith, Perth, Sunshine Coast, Sydney, Tamworth, Toowoomba, Wagga Wagga, Wollongong.

Internet Service Providers Tel: 1800 240 399
Email: info@isp.com.au
Areas covered: Adelaide, Albury, Bairnsdale, Ballarat, Bathurst, Bendigo, Brisbane, Bundaberg, Cairns, Canberra, Conbram, Darwin, Echuca, Geelong, Gladstone, Gosford, Hamilton, Hobart, Kyneton, Launceston, Mackay, Maroochydore, Melbourne, Mildura, Moe, Newcastle, Perth, Portland, Rockhampton, Rosebud, Sale, Shepparton, Southport, Sydney, Toowoomba, Townsville, Wangaratta, Warrnambool, Whyalla, Wodonga, Wollongong.

Net-Trek Australia Tel: (07) 5526 4655
Email: simon@mars.nettrek.net.au
Areas covered: Adelaide, Brisbane, Canberra, Gold Coast, Hobart, Melbourne, Sydney, various regional centres.

OzEmail Tel: 1800 805 874 Email: sales@ozemail.com.au
Areas covered: Adelaide, Albury, Alice Springs, Armidale, Brisbane, Broken Hill, Bundaberg, Cairns, Campbelltown, Canberra, Coffs Harbour, Darwin, Dubbo, Geelong, Gold Coast, Gosford, Goulburn, Griffith, Hobart, Lismore, Lithgow, Mackay, Melbourne, Newcastle, Nowra, Orange, Penrith, Perth, Port Macquarie, Rockhampton, Sunshine Coast, Sydney, Tamworth, Taree, Toowoomba, Townsville, Wagga Wagga, Wollongong.

Pegasus Networks Tel: (07) 3259 6259

Email: sales@pegasus.net.au

Areas covered: Adelaide, Albury, Armidale, Bathurst, Brisbane, Bundaberg, Campbelltown, Canberra, Dalby, Darwin, Gosford, Gunnedah, Gympie, Hobart, Katoomba, Kingaroy, Lismore, Mackay, Maryborough, Melbourne, Moree, Narrabri, Nowra, Orange, Penrith, Perth, Sunshine Coast, Sydney, Tamworth, Toowoomba, Wagga Wagga, Wollongong.

Ruralnet Australia Tel: (03) 5021 0150

Email: info@rural.net.net.au

Areas covered: Annuella, Bannerton, Bendigo, Birchip, Boort, Boundary Bend, Broken Hill, Buronga, Cardross, Charlton, Cockburn, Colignan, Curlwaa, Dareton, Donald, Euston, Gol Gol, Irymple, Kerang, Korong Vale, Menindee, Merbein, Mildura, Nangiloc, Nichols Point, Olary, Ouyen, Pyramid Hill, Robinvale, St Arnaud, Swan Hill.

Rural Press Limited Tel: 1800 809 164

Email: support@rpl.com.au

Areas covered: Adelaide, Albury, Bairnsdale, Ballarat, Bendigo, Brisbane, Bundaberg, Cairns, Canberra, Darwin, Geelong, Gosford, Hamilton, Hobart, Launceston, Maroochydore, Melbourne, Mildura, Perth, Rockhampton, Rosebud, Sale, Shepparton, Southport, Sydney, Toowoomba, Townsville, Wangaratta, Whyalla, Wodonga, Wollongong.

Starway Corporation Tel: 1800 242 020

Email: info@starway.net.au

Areas covered: Ballarat, Brisbane, Canberra, Geelong, Gold Coast, Melbourne, Mornington Peninsula, Sydney, Wollongong.

Telstra Big Pond Tel: 1800 804 282 Email: info@bigpond.com

Areas covered: Telstra has local connections Australia-wide, and in all capital cities. Check your local phone book, or send an e-mail message.

Wantree Internet Tel: (08) 9211 8899 Email: info@wantree.com.au

Areas covered: Adelaide, Perth.

Zip Internet Professionals Tel: 1300 655 577

Email: info@zip.com.au

Areas covered: Camden, Campbelltown, Gosford, Helensburgh, Mulgoa, Penrith, Sydney, Windsor, Wisemans Ferry.

Glossary

ASCII American Standard Code for Information Interchange; an ASCII file is a common way of transferring files across the Internet as plain text. In your word processor, choose 'File Save As', and you will be given the ASCII (text) option. It's a way of sending your information to someone who uses different software from you.

applet A small, self-contained application, running alone or inside another software program.

attachment A file attached to e-mail, usually attached in the format it was created in. This is an easy way of sending word processor, spreadsheet and other files across the Internet.

backbone The primary high-speed Internet links between a country's major ISPs.

baud A modem speed measurement of signals per second.

BBS Bulletin Board System. A local computer acting as a message board, often offered by commercial companies as a service or after-sales service facility. You can dial into the computer and download or upload files, and leave messages for others, such as service personnel or other users of the BBS.

binary file A file which contains pure data, such as a software program.

bit A binary unit.

bmp A bitmap; a graphics file format.

bps Bits per second, used to indicate data transfer rates of a modem; also Kbps, Kilobits per second, and Mbps, megabits per second.

broadband High bandwidth networks, transferring data at a speed greater than 256 Kbps.

cache A memory storage area for regularly accessed or recently used data.

client An individual computer; may also refer to the software program it uses to request data from a server computer and program.

compression Making files smaller by removing all the bits not needed. Compression is used when archiving data, or when transferring it to another computer.

cookie A packet of data stored on your computer or Web site which is sent back to the Web server which installed it when it's requested.

cross-posting When used in Usenet, it means a posting (message) sent to several newsgroups at once.

domain Part of the Internet address hierarchy of a machine. For example, yourcompanyname.com.au, is 'yourcompanyname', a commercial site in the Australian domain.

download Retrieving or copying information from another computer on the network. The opposite of upload.

emoticons Smileys :), and other text icons which are supposed to indicate your state of mind. Emoticons are not usually used when sending business communications.

encryption A method of encoding data for secrecy, so that it can only be read by the people for whom it is intended.

FAQ Frequently Asked Questions. These files are often kept by Usenet newsgroups and mailing lists. They're meant to answer questions commonly asked by newcomers. You should always check the FAQ file before you post a message to a newsgroup or a mailing list.

F2F Face to face. A common acronym used in newsgroups to denote an actual meeting.

FIF Fractal Image Format. An image compression and display format which offers a 50:1 compression, with view-zoom capabilities for the graphics.

firewall Network hardware and software which limits access to and from the Internet from an internal network or computer.

flame A term often used in Usenet or in mailing lists. An angry exchange or response.

freeware Software and utilities which are made freely available by the author. Although you don't have to pay for the program, it is nevertheless still covered by the author's copyright.

FTP File Transfer Protocol. A system for delivering files across computer networks.

gateway A machine which is connected to two networks. It acts as an information transfer point.

GIF Graphics Interchange Format. A format for graphics which is often used on the World Wide Web.

gopher An information retrieval system which 'burrows' through menus.

GUI Graphic User Interface—for example, Microsoft Windows.

header The top of an e-mail or newsgroup message, showing where a message originated and when it was posted.

HTML HyperText Markup Language. Tags added to information so that it can be viewed across the Web and linked with other information.

hyperlink A spot on a Web page which links it to another Web page or Web site.

hypertext Text which includes hyperlinks to other documents.

imagemap Menu options and links which are part of a graphic image.

IRC Internet Relay Chat. Text-based communication popular across the Internet.

ISDN Integrated Services Digital Network. Uses phone lines and computer networks to provide telecommunications—video, voice and data.

ISP Internet Service Provider.

JPEG Joint Photographic Experts Group. An image compression and display method. A common graphics format across the Web because image files can be compressed 20:1. If you have a graphics program, it will usually be able to convert your image files to JPEG.

LAN Local Area Network. Computers joined via cables, usually within the same building.

mailing list A list of subscribers to a discussion group. All subscribers receive all messages via e-mail. A mailing list may also be used to distribute a newsletter.

Majordomo A popular mailing list administration program.

MIDI Musical Instrument Digital Interface. A standard protocol for synthesizers and computers, allowing them to communicate.

mirror site A site which contains the same information as another site elsewhere on the Internet. Mirroring to other sites is used for popular sites to limit the amount of traffic to a particular site.

modem Modulator/demodulator. A device which converts signals to analogue and vice versa, distributing data across phone lines.

moderator A person who monitors a newsgroup or a mailing list, ensuring that all postings are relevant before posting them.

newsgroup A discussion list on a particular topic, part of Usenet.

nodename The name of a machine on a network.

NNTP Net News Transfer Protocol. The transmission protocol for Usenet.

PGP Pretty Good Privacy. An encryption program which allows you to encode your data for secrecy when you transmit it across the Internet.

plug-in An add-on feature for your browser which increases the browser's features.

POP Point of Presence. As used by ISPs, it means giving local access to a network. It can also mean Post Office Protocol, when used in reference to an e-mail program.

PPP Point to Point Protocol. A direct connection to the Internet from your PC, via a modem and telephone line.

proxy A machine used as a storage area for commonly accessed files. Used to speed up transfer of information from the Internet.

RAM Random Access Memory. The amount of memory in your computer available to programs.

ROM Read-Only Memory.

router A device used to transfer information packets from a computer on a LAN to other networks.

search engine A computer program which searches indexes of Internet addresses using keywords.

server Any computer which stores information and makes it available to users.

shareware Copyrighted software programs publicly distributed and available for users to trial. If users continue to use a program, they are required to send a payment to the author.

SMTP Simple Mail Transfer Protocol. A transfer method for e-mail on the Internet.

spam Unsolicited advertising sent via e-mail or posted to newsgroups.

TCP/IP Transmission Control Protocol/Internet Protocol. A combination of networking protocols used by computers to communicate over the Internet.

TIFF Tagged Image File Format. A common graphics file format.

URL Uniform Resource Locator. The address system used on the Web.

Usenet The network of discussion groups on the Internet.

VRML Virtual Reality Modelling Language. A programming language for the creation of virtual environments. If you add a VRML accessory to your browser, you can explore virtual environments, such as a 3D model of a building.

WAN Wide Area Network. A number of computers separated by distance, but joined via dedicated lines.

WYSIWYG What You See Is What You Get. Often used to refer to HTML authoring programs which insert the HTML code for you; you see the page as it will appear in your browser.

Index

address book, 5, 7, 120
advertising, 74–5, 85, 92–6
    jobs, 167
    on newsgroups, 115
AltaVista, 14, 69, 70
Amazon.com, 108
America Online, 2, 4
announcements (Web site), 54
appointments, 17, 22
audio, 64
autoresponder, 91–2, 98

banks, 155–7
banner ads, 66, 94, 98
brainstorm, 48
budget, 26, 39, 66
business
    cycle, 87–9
    definition, 26–7
    plan, 29
    writing, 124–6

chat software, xiii, 90
chatting, 89–91

classified ads, 30, 84, 92, 97–8
clients, 36
communications, viii
competitors, 42
CompuServe, 2, 4
contact
    lists, 7
    management checklist, 120
    software, 120
contacts, 62, 118–30
    company, 139–40
cookies, 63, 81
cool site, 134–5
credentials, 23
customers, 8, 16, 24, 28, 109
    expectations, 45
    needs, 49
    service, 18
cybermall, 32, 33, 35–6, 46

DejaNews, 105
direct mail, 102–3
direct marketing, 85–6
discounts, 20